HOW THE WORLD ENDS

UNDERSTANDING THE GROWING CHAOS

J.B. SHREVE

WINDMILL MEDIA

Cover design by Miles D. Mungo

HOW THE WORLD ENDS

UNDERSTANDING THE GROWING CHAOS

J.B. Shreve

A debt of gratitude is owed to many people who participated and tolerated the process of developing this book.

To my wife Casie and our children, thank you for allowing me to talk about this for the past four years. Thank you for the early mornings and afternoons spent in front of the computer as I researched and developed the pages that follow.

To Jessica and Terry, thank you for catching so many mistakes and problems in the early drafts. Thanks for helping to make my thoughts make sense.

To my good friend and kindred spirit Mike Schultz, thank you for the many conversations and encouragements that served as the seeds for nearly every chapter in this book.

To the men of Hebron Company in Fayetteville, Arkansas, thank you for being part of the Ark that will preserve our homes in the rising chaos of this generation.

INTRODUCTION

One afternoon in 2015 I happened to be watching the news and saw images of the red rafts full of refugees who were moving across the Mediterranean toward Europe. These were refugees from the wars and violence of the Middle East and North Africa. Many of the rafts were upending at sea and the would-be refugees were dying. In other instances, the rafts were being intercepted by authorities and the people returned to their lands of departure. As a result of this, the refugees were becoming the human inventory for a burgeoning slave and sex trafficking trade out of North Africa.

The politics of Europe were in a state of massive upheaval, largely in response to the refugee crisis. Several European countries were looking to nationalist candidates in the upcoming elections thanks to rising xenophobia. This was before Brexit. France, contrary to its proud history of liberal democracy, was outlawing the public use of religious symbols on one's attire to combat the burka among Muslim immigrants entering the country.

I knew enough about the refugee crisis to recognize Europe was barely being impacted by this event compared to nations like Turkey, Lebanon and others who sat at the borders of the nations that were bleeding displaced people that summer.

And the refugee crisis was only one of the multiple parts of chaos afflicting the globe at that time. I released a podcast series on the civil war in Syria and another about the collapse of the Middle East around this time. In Venezuela, the once prosperous nation was collapsing. Corruption was wrecking Brazil's economy and political system.

As I watched video footage of this raft full of refugees move across the Mediterranean Sea and contemplated all of the chaos occurring in the world at that time, the thought hit me, this is like a disaster movie! In this light the refugees are our characters jumping from the Titanic or racing away from the exploding volcano. The scenes of this disaster movie have only worsened since that time. And once you see our modern chaotic global landscape in this light, you cannot un-see it.

That is where this book comes from. It is from a realization that much of the media, much of our politics, and much of our local-based perspectives keep us from seeing the weight of what is taking shape today. Once we finally see it, the natural questions we respond with include, why is this happening and what do we need to do about it? As I dug into the research regarding the many different crises impacting the globe in the years since 2015, I identified three core crises: population, food and water. All of these areas of the world where chaos is the most overwhelming today are being pummeled by these three root issues. But as the chaos works out from these societies, it morphs and takes the form of newer crises and chaos. Examples of these newly formed byproduct crises include terrorism, refugees, disease, and many other issues that are not confined to the lands where population, food, and water crises are most severe. These are the means by which the chaos is spreading across the globe.

This is the story I share in the pages of this book. This is a story about how the world is coming undone and far from a search for solutions, I contend it is too late to do much to stop this unfolding chaos. It is only going to get worse. Civilization as we know it cannot go on for another fifty years. This is not a prediction. It is a simple assessment of the spreading chaos already racing through the global system and order.

This book was designed to stand on its own. The research, the facts, the honest and non-political focus which I offer to readers was meant to break through our polarized perspectives of the day and warn about what is coming. It was meant to give my reader an understanding of the chaos taking shape in the world today and supply readers with the knowledge needed to develop their own worldviews independent of polarized and politically biased agendas so rampant in our culture today.

But I could not stop there. As I recognized the underlying systemic flaws that are at the root of the modern chaos of our world and which explain so much of the collapse we are experiencing, I also began to see other more important trends. The core drivers moving us toward global collapse are not political ideologies, climate change, or natural disasters. When we dig all the way to the bottom of the chaos, we find the corrupted heart of man.

My original intent was not to write a book that included insight into my personal faith or even the utilization of scripture. It was meant to stand alone as a nonfiction analysis and explainer discussing what is going on in the world today. I wanted to help readers better understand the world. But the deeper I got into my exploration of the issues, the more difficult I found it to separate them from the truth. The system is corrupt because the heart of man is corrupt.

To that end, this book is a perspective drawn from my own worldview. It is not designed to be preachy or insist this is the only correct perspective out there. My hope is that readers will be empowered in these pages through knowledge, analysis and educated insight to develop their own worldviews.

A Word on Worldviews

There is an erroneous assumption in our society that worldviews derived from a primarily spiritual outlook upon life are illegitimate. The reality is that a host of inputs contribute to every person's perspective of the world, even if many are unaware of the impact of those inputs. The spiritual basis for my own worldview, and that shared by many Christian believers today, is a deliberate selection of the philosophical inputs that contribute to how we see the world. There are many leaders, statesmen, and philosophers in our generation who make deliberate selections of the philosophical inputs that contribute to how they see the world. I contend the basis for their worldviews are far more fragile than a worldview built upon the values clarified in the Bible.

In 2008, at the height of the economic meltdown, former Federal Reserve Chairman Alan Greenspan sat before a United States Congress committee and explained his own confusion at what was taking place. "I made a mistake in presuming that the self-interests of organizations, specifically banks and others, were such as that they were best capable of protecting their own shareholders and their equity in the firms," Mr. Greenspan said. "I have found a flaw. I don't know how significant or permanent it is. But I have been very distressed by that fact." Political leaders and bureaucrats seldom confess to error. In response, Congressman Waxman sought clarification from Mr. Greenspan. "In other words, you found that your view of the world, your ideology, was not right, it was not working," Mr. Waxman said. "Absolutely, precisely," Greenspan replied. "You know, that's precisely the reason I was shocked, because I have been going for 40 years or more with very considerable evidence that it was working exceptionally well."[1]

What was Mr. Greenspan's worldview? Free markets and capitalism were a big part of it, but Greenspan was also a lifelong disciple of Ayn Rand. This was the philosophical input that contributed to the development of his worldview. He was part of the philosopher and author's inner circle when she was alive. Followers of Rand, known as Objectivists, believe in the power of individual strength. They believe charity is pointless, even stupid. Right and wrong are defined by anything that frees or limits individual expression and fulfillment.

In 2019, a Democratic candidate for the presidency, Marianne Williamson attributed the problems in America to "dark psychic forces" at work in the American culture. She was described in the New Yorker in this way:

"Williamson, a nondenominational psycho-spiritual leader, who mixes references to Christianity with quotes from philosophers, Martin Luther King, Jr., and Deepak Chopra, has based her Presidential candidacy on an unspoken premise: that the country might be experiencing an epidemic of mental illness. Actually, it's not that unspoken: "We have a problem with the psychological fabric of our country," a section on her campaign Web site, titled "The Issues Aren't Always the Issue," says. "A low level emotional civil war has begun in too many ways to rip us apart."[2]

We all have worldviews and the facts, revelations, experience and other contributors that help shape that worldview vary. In the end, the strength and validity of a worldview should not be measured by its popularity or the lack thereof but by its merits. What does your worldview build and how does it endure in both the short-term and the long-term? To that end:

*I am not ashamed of the Gospel. I see it as the very power of God working for the salvation of everyone who believes it...**Romans 1:16** (Phillips Translation)*

My hope is that this book will empower you to see the world differently. That means also seeing the growing chaos across the globe differently. In the place of complacency, fear, or anxiety, I hope you will find knowledge, understanding and purpose. Most importantly, it is my hope that people of faith will take confidence in the midst of the growing chaos, their minds enlightened with understanding, and seek out a deeper partnership with God that is needed in this pivotal day.

JB Shreve, September 15, 2019

---

1. **CSPAN.** *Waxman and Greenspan on Ideology.* https://www.c-span.org/video/?
c4535454/waxman-greenspan-ideology, 2008.

2. **Witt, Emily.** The New Yorker. *Marianne Williamson Wants Politics to Enter the New
Age.* [Online] August 14, 2019. [Cited: September 14, 2019.] https://www.
newyorker.com/news/news-desk/marianne-williamson-wants-politics-to-enter-
the-new-age.

7 OBJECTIVES OF THIS BOOK

By the end of this book the following objectives should be achieved among the readers.

1. **You will better understand the scale of the chaos engulfing our world.** This is unlike anything we have ever seen, and you will recognize that fact when you pay attention to the news after reading this book. You are going to be more aware than most of your friends and peers.

2. **You will better understand that the reality behind the chaos is often more than what is reported in our sound bite media culture today.** There are deeper issues at work. You will begin to see those issues for yourself. The facts that are reported, usually do not accurately reflect the bigger picture and the fuller story.

3. **You will understand how the world works and why the growing chaos is evidence of the world no longer working.** Systems are indeed already collapsing, and you will see this for yourself.

4. **Because you understand what is taking place today, you**

will be able to develop your own educated worldview and perspective. This worldview will help you better defend yourself and your home from confusion and fear brought on by the increasing chaos.

5. **You will see the deeper impact of the corrupted human heart that is taking a toll on the collapsing systems of the earth.** The global order is not being destroyed by an external force. It is self-destructing.

6. **You will begin to see there is a competing design for life and the world, ordained by God, that is in opposition to the world systems and order that are collapsing today.** This God ordained design for life and society is strong and impervious to the growing chaos.

7. **You will be equipped to seek the design of God for yourself and your home and build a response system that can hold strong in the face of the growing chaos.** This is not achieved on an individual level alone. It is accomplished in the company of your Christian brothers and sisters.

All scriptural references in this book are using the New International Version unless otherwise specified.

PART I

THIS IS THE WAY THE WORLD ENDS

This is the way the world ends
  This is the way the world ends
  This is the way the world ends
  Not with a bang but a whimper.
  T.S. Eliot "The Hollow Men"

1

THE END

September 2, 2015. Under cover of an early morning dawn a young Kurdish family, the Kurdis, crowds onto a small inflatable boat on a beach in Turkey. They are fleeing the violent war that recently enveloped their homeland in Syria. Crouched alongside them in the boat as they cast off is an assortment of strangers. The boat's occupants are united only in their flight. They are part of a historic flow of refugees across the globe. Millions are running from violence, poverty, and unprecedented humanitarian crises and systemic global chaos. The Kurdi family's ultimate destination is Canada where they have relatives who can house them and provide much needed sanctuary. If they can get to Europe, perhaps they can then find a way to North America. This morning's journey is the next leg of their exodus.

But they will not make it to Europe. The Kurdi family members are not the main characters in this story. They are background images, running from the chaos as fast as they can before it finally and inevitably consumes them.

They are only at the beginning of the journey to Greece on this morning when their boat capsizes. Rihanna, the mother of the Kurdi family drowns. We don't know whether she lived to see her son,

Ghalib, sink under the water for the last time when he also drowned. The youngest, three-year-old Aylan, probably perished before both of them. His tiny 3-year-old body sank quickly in the waters of the Mediterranean Sea. It's not known if he even knew how to swim before embarking on the treacherous voyage.

The Kurdi family was only a small piece of the anonymous 3,600 refugees who died in the eastern Mediterranean Sea in 2015. We don't know the other stories. Most of us will never know their names. We only know the Kurdi family because images of the toddler's body, washed onto the shores of Greece, happened to be captured. The tiny lifeless body was still wearing his blue shorts. A fitted red shirt. Small toddler shoes. His soaked body was asleep forever. Aylan Kurdi washed up with the tide like waste from a passing ship. The image spread around the world to remind the rest of us what was going on over there. Aylan was memorialized in multiple outlets as part of the 2015 year in pictures. Then we moved on.

It Is Getting Worse

Tragedy. Chaos. Death. Crisis. Everywhere we look today our perspectives are bombarded with these terrible and frequently confusing realities. Even the way we interpret what we observe has become part of the growing chaos and disaster, changing the shape and nature of our governments, our societies, and our worldview. But the real story is not the tragic events. It is not even the people being consumed by these events. The real story is larger. It is global. It is a worldwide reckoning that the end of the world is now unfolding.

A three-year-old's body washes ashore on an idyllic beach in southern Europe. His drowned, lifeless corpse is a discarded fragment of the chaos moving north from the Middle East and North Africa, where mobs of refugees are fleeing their homelands. Across the globe from Asia to Central and South America, the roads, waterways, and borderlands are flooded with hordes of refugees fleeing for their lives. In the US, armed guards defend the border against caravans of immigrants who also marched across countries, only to face confrontation here as well. Children are separated from their parents and both are placed in holding centers enclosed with barbed wire at the southern border of the land of the free and home of the brave.

When we take the time to look around, it is not difficult to observe unprecedented chaos in every corner of the world. In the world's leading cities, such as Paris, London, Cairo, Nairobi, Mumbai and more, bombs ignite, fires burn, gunshots ring out, and the cries and screams of victims alert the world to new terror attacks. Some of the attacks are carried out by members of the same bands of refugees who sought shelter behind the borders of these nations and lands. In other instances, the perpetrators are home grown fanatics consumed with an irrational and ungodly religious fervor aimed at self and societal destruction. Their only consistent uniting factor is an all-consuming hunger for death and its spread.

In central Africa, an Ebola outbreak spreads. The doctors are present. The international aid organizations are present. But both are consistently attacked by the locals who do not trust them. Order is breaking down in areas where it was only held in place by a thread to begin with. In other parts of the world, diseases like cholera and measles, which were once considered eradicated, are making a comeback. The cures are present, but the levels of widespread social distrust nullify their implementation and usefulness.

Meanwhile, the United Nations alerts the world that famine threatens 20 million people from Africa to the Middle East. Mothers in Yemen are incapable of nursing their infants because their own bodies are so malnourished by starvation. Parents must choose whether to take an injured child to the hospital or to pay for a small meal for their other child who is not injured. All the while, this scene plays out in a war zone no one is paying attention to. More than 70,000 have been killed as victims to the conflict in Yemen since 2015.

A post-apocalyptic group rises from the ashes of war in Iraq and Syria. They call themselves The Caliphate, but the world knows them as ISIS. Across the region they begin a reign of unprecedented terror. Genocide barely defines what they achieve. As one town and city after another falls to their conquest, the local men are rounded up and executed; their mass graves will be discovered periodically for years to come. The older women, wives, and mothers are sold as slaves, erased from any record of existence. The younger women become the spoils of war for the militants. Rape, slavery, crucifixion, and other mass atrocities mark the trail of onslaught traveled by this brutal group. In West Africa, a copycat group rises. They are Boko Haram, and they soon pledge their allegiance to ISIS. Their methods include suicide bombings, executions by chainsaw, and the kidnapping of hundreds of schoolgirls hidden in the forests and hideaways of these maniacs.

We have seen violence and atrocities before, but the consistency and global reach of today's brutalities is unprecedented. Genocide in South Asia. Child soldiers in the Democratic Republic of the Congo. Rape warfare in South Sudan. In Indonesia an entire family commits suicide terrorist attacks on multiple targets. This includes the mother, father and children as young as 9 years old. Today's societies are routinely concocting new depravities to which they can sink.

Across the world, China has placed more than 1 million members of an ethnic group into "education" camps. Children of these prisoners are sent to hidden centers and taught that their parents are insane because of their religious beliefs. The United Nations, due to divides and bickering among its members, barely discusses what is occurring.

In South Africa, day zero is announced. It is the day when the nation officially runs out of water. Less than a thousand miles away in Mozambique, cyclones lash the land with rain and flooding devastates the country. More than a thousand are killed. Billions of dollars in damages have crippled the nation. In one part of the continent people are parched. In another part of the continent they drown.

In Algeria, a dictator is removed. In Egypt, a dictator is secured. Inflation rises to 800% in Venezuela. The world's largest dust bowl takes shape in China as poor soil management upends the agricultural efforts and deserts begin to expand. In India, a suicide epidemic has taken hold of the nation's small farmers who would rather die than face the shame of their failures as their way of life is consumed by the modern global food system.

Earthquakes in Pakistan and Iran.

Mudslides in Japan, Indonesia and California.

Domestic unrest shakes the nations of the world.

Political revolutions. Geopolitical gridlock.

Anger among the voters.

Brexit. Trump. Arab Spring.

African Spring.

The ascent of nationalism in western democracies not seen since before World War 2.

Coups.

Revolutions.

Antifa. Alt Right.

The rise of authoritarian leaders.

These are not scenes from a disaster movie. These are the scenes from our news headlines since 2015. They are the scenes of a world system coming undone. They are the images and headlines of a global system in a state of collapse. This is what it looks like when the world as we know it is coming undone. This is the unfolding historical record of how the world ends.

FOR THE PAST decade I have observed and recorded the growing levels of chaos around the world. I secured degrees in International Relations and Middle East Studies after the 9/11 attacks. I began my masters work in Global Business around the time of the economic meltdown in 2008. Something was happening. This was more than history. It was moving too fast for mere history. The way the world works was changing. In fact, the way the world works was actually no longer working at all. In 2012 I began documenting my observations through a web site and podcast, www.TheEndOfHistory.net. Meanwhile, the pace of increasing global dysfunction intensified. No system of global civilization was immune from this chaos. Crisis has become our new normal to such an extent that it barely registers as an alarm when we hear about the next crisis in the news.

This book is not written to persuade the reader to any political cause or agenda. It is meant to recalibrate the way we view the world and the chaos unfolding all around us. We are taught and trained to see this chaos through a political framework or through the distance of "over there" and "those people." These views are incorrect. The frequency and scale of the growing crisis is already beginning to overwhelm such paradigms, leading to growing confusion and crisis fatigue. We are witnessing the beginning of the end. It is not something we can prevent. It has already begun. Recognizing this reality will change the way we interpret current events and perhaps make the acceleration of chaos more predictable and less disorienting.

This book is divided into five parts. Part one explores the reality of our current predicament, separate from the familiar narratives and political agendas. Parts two, three, and four examine foundational components of our global system: population, food, and water. These fractured foundations are already stretched too far beyond repair. When we understand how these foundational components of the global system are collapsing, then we will better understand that much of the chaos we are experiencing today is an effect, not a cause, of the global disaster. For example, rising levels of terrorism, war, and even refugee flows can all be traced back to the scarcity of space, food, and water among the world's poorest populations. While the poorest nations of the world may be the current hot spots for chaos, the interconnectedness of the global system assures the chaos will, and indeed has already begun to, spread to the richer nations of the world. The fights and policies to prevent the spread of this chaos from a global system in collapse will define the news and political narratives of the next fifty years.

Part five will explore the political paralysis and divisions across the globe which will accelerate and polarize into growing authoritarianism. The deficient systems of leadership and government across the planet will not only fail to stop the spread of our current global collapse, but they will actually play a role in intensifying and accelerating the growth of chaos and crisis. Finally, the concluding chapters will examine the underlying, hidden realities of the world -- universal principles, if you will -- whose violation assures the continued rise of chaos.

This is how the world ends, and this is the explanation for the chaos of the world all around us!

2

REMEMBERING THE LAST TIME THE WORLD ENDED

When I reference the "end of the world," I am not suggesting an impending extinction-level event (ELE) often popularized in Hollywood's disaster movies. The world is not going to end upon impact from a giant meteor or a sudden ice age. In fact, the end of the world is not coming about by any single event. It will come about by multiple events and, more importantly, brought on by multiple sources. The end of the world I am referring to is a great convergence of crises, both natural and manmade, each compounding in their scope and scale as they crash into one another like terrible calamitous waves of tragedy and disaster. The convergence of these crises into one another will be the unfolding of human history over the next 50 years. The distinctions between cause and effect will be lost as our systems, cultures, and civilization roil under the traumatizing effects of this chaos.

We have seen the end of the world before. Leading figures and thinkers in the early 5th century viewed the fall of Rome to the barbarians as an apocalyptic event. One of those thinkers, St. Augustine, wrote *The City of God* as an account of his realization that perhaps the purposes of God involved more than Rome as the center of the modern world. As civilization collapsed all around him, the pagans argued that the gods had brought about the end of the world because of Rome's conversion to Christianity. Augustine countered that the end of Rome was not the end of God's purposes, but the separation of a city of the damned from the eternal City of God. A whole theology upon which many of the governments of the middle ages were based came from Augustine's revelation as the end of the world in his generation unfolded.

Much later in history in the 13th century, Baghdad was the center of the modern world and the pinnacle of Islam's golden age. Internal decay and corruption were already a leading concern for those living within the great city, and they feared what the future held for them. Leading nobles and residents within the city and government warned that their government and leadership had gone astray and drifted from the foundations that originally made their culture so grand. Their warnings went unheeded, and by the middle of the century this human civilization was brought to an end as the Mongol Horde swept over the city. Baghdad was only a piece of the 12 million square miles of conquest achieved by the Mongols. In almost every city laid siege to by the Mongols, the buildings were burned to the ground and the people were executed or sold into slavery. It is estimated that as much as 5% of the world's population was destroyed by the Mongol advance. The power of Asia which had ruled the world since the fall of Rome was ended, and Europe ascended into modern history. This was the end of the world for a once great civilization.

In the 14th century, the Black Death decimated the globe. As many as one hundred million people died around the world. Europe's population alone was reduced by 30-60%. The Catholic Church and the kings of Europe proved powerless to stop the spread of the plague, and villages lined their streets with the corpses of dead loved ones for the undertaker to carry away. Those living at the time, whether common or elite, weak or powerful, were impotent in the face of this spreading death. The artwork of the period is infested with skulls and images of the Angel of Death as the people living in the chaos knew they were experiencing the apocalypse and the end of the world.

In the Western Hemisphere, great civilizations and cultures grew independently from the old worlds of Asia and Europe. The cities and economies of the empires of the Mayans, Incas, and the Aztecs dwarfed the mightiest civilizations of Europe in the era before they were discovered by Europe. Yet they were annihilated by European diseases, conquest, and internal collapse in the span of a century. Their sparse records and architecture, along with the conqueror's records of their extermination, became all that was left to tell about a once great civilization before the end of their world arrived.

Warning Cries

In every instance when the world has ended for history's expired civilizations, there were voices of warnings and pathways offered to avert destruction. These were often lone voices who went against the flow and standards of the times they lived in. Their alarm and concern frequently forced them to the fringe of their decaying civilizations. They were seen as doomsday prophets, naysayers, and contrarians. Throughout history, their warnings were never heeded, and destruction was never averted. This is the historical pattern which we are once again following today. Accompanying the growing warnings from groups like the United Nations and the world's scientists about what our civilization will face in the next half-century, there are instructions as to what our societies and leaders can do to avert the impending disasters. Like the people of prior eras of humanity, from the elite of Baghdad to the nobles of the Incas, these warnings are not being heeded and the steps to avert disaster are not being followed.

It is already too late! The warning cries of the world's scientists and leading bodies will continue to grow louder and more frequent as the evidence of the end of our world continues to mount, but the time to heed warnings and implement solutions has in fact already passed. The undoing has already begun. It is occurring all around us, but we do not recognize it as such. The names of great wars and great tragedies in history are not assigned by their victims. The survivors who rebuild in the aftermath assign these names. It is the survivors who record the history. It is the victims who suffer the end of the world, usually without understanding what is happening.

Regarding False Prophets

As a Christian, thoughts about the end of the world are not foreign. A belief in the end of time and the return of Christ is central to my faith. It is also a personal frustration when I survey the culture of modern Christianity. When I observe modern Christianity's perspective of the end of the world, apocalypse, and eschatology it is confusing and frequently weird.

When I was a young teenager first learning to drive a flyer was placed on my windshield informing me that the world was going to end in 1992. The announcement concerned me. A large part of me knew it was not true. These predictions were never true. These predictions were whacky. At the local Christian bookstore one author explained that Saddam Hussein was the anti-Christ and America was initiating the apocalypse by going to war with Iraq. This was during the time of the first Gulf War in 1991. Another author offered a book *88 Reasons Jesus Is Coming Back in 1988.* We were four years past that prophetic due date and it still wasn't true. Somehow no one ever denounced these authors as false prophets and the genre was always prominently displayed at the bookstore.

But what if it was true? What if 1992 was the time that it really happened? The Bible says no man knows the day or the hour, not even the angels in heaven (Matthew 24:36). But with so many predictions, even a broken clock is right twice a day, and someone will eventually get this right even if only by accident. What if it was this time? Was I ready? A short term personal spiritual revival sparked in me for the duration of the summer of 1992 - only to fade by the beginning of the school year. This wasn't the time. This wasn't real.

That is the problem throughout the history of religion. Our understanding of the end of time becomes encased in a personal filter that frequently does not fit the reality God is working out historically. The religious leaders in first century Jerusalem anticipated a

Messiah who would come as a military or political leader. When Jesus arrived as a carpenter's son, one who socialized with prostitutes and tax collectors, it was impossible for them to believe this was the fulfillment of God's promises. Christians, the most expert among them, frequently miss the unfolding purposes of God because it does not match their own expectations. This is a historical pattern.

> *Jesus answered: "Watch out that no one deceives you. For many will come in my name, claiming, 'I am the Messiah,' and will deceive many. You will hear of wars and rumors of wars, but see to it that you are not alarmed. Such things must happen, but the end is still to come. Nation will rise against nation, and kingdom against kingdom. There will be famines and earthquakes in various places. All these are the beginning of birth pains.* **Matthew 24:4-8**

Every American incursion into the Middle East in my lifetime has included an upsurge of Christian preachers and pundits predicting this is the beginning of the end of the world. They are always wrong. They are always wrong because they usually don't understand global politics and the Middle East. Frankly, they don't really understand the Bible either. There have always been wars and rumors of war. That is what Jesus is literally saying in this passage from Matthew. *You will hear of wars and rumors of wars, but see to it that you are not alarmed. Such things must happen,* **but the end is still to come.** We frequently misplace our local politics and perspectives with God's global purposes.

Because of this frequent error in Christianity I have been deliberately cautious when it comes to including a Biblical worldview into the pages of this book. An earlier draft of the book in fact was written entirely without any reference to faith or scripture. This book was meant to stand alone as a study on global affairs and the growing levels of chaos and disaster across the planet. The premise that we are living at the end of the world is not offered as a way to prove the Bible is true here. The last thing I want to write is another doomsday book like the false prophets I remember from my childhood. At the same time, when we look at the state of the world today we cannot escape the facts of systemic collapse that bombard us. Things are falling apart. This will be demonstrated in the pages of this book with facts and case studies from around the world. The world system as we know it simply cannot endure another fifty years.

When Jesus spoke of the end of the world the most consistent elements of his warnings were "do not fear" and "do not be deceived." He makes those warnings repeatedly. The intent of this book is to help readers understand the growing chaos all around us. This will aid in preventing deception. In the end, I hope to also provide hope. Things are bad and they are going to get much worse. People of faith can take hope however. They do not need to fear. This is how the world ends and this is how we can make sense of our context and the posture we should hold in the midst of the chaos.

3

THE LAST GENERATION

The world as we know it cannot endure the next half century. The chaos unfolding all around us today is the beginning of the great undoing and collapse of modern human civilization. In the next 50 years, our way of life will come to an end. What we are witnessing is not a fight for survival but evidence of the incredible vulnerability of our global system and civilization.

Scientists from around the world and across varying fields of expertise are increasingly warning of a "sixth mass extinction" currently taking shape. The earth has experienced five mass extinctions in its history, and the current one is unfolding at a much faster rate than what the fossil record demonstrates concerning those prior events[1]. Mass extinctions do not include our own species alone. Up to 1 million species are at risk of annihilation, many of these within decades, according to a 2019 report from the Intergovernmental Science-Policy Platform on Biodiversity and Ecosystem Services[2]. As these species die off, the overall ecosystem and our civilization's food and water supplies will be significantly impacted. Our national government and international institutions lack the resolve and leadership necessary for preventing this global collapse. As the dire predictions of experts manifest into our present daily realities, most of mankind will be unable to adapt to the confounding changes.

A 2018 report from the United Nations Panel on Climate Change[3] warned of worsening food shortages, coastal flooding, and wildfires by 2040. The report was written by 91 scientists from 40 countries around the world. These trends, according to the UN report, will take the most significant toll on the world's poor and desperate who are often housed in the most threatened geographic zones. These will be the first victims, but they will not be the last. Across the globe we now have "seasons" for hurricanes, typhoons, wildfires, and monsoons. In 2018, natural disasters cost the world $155 billion[4], fourteen times what the US budget allotted to food and agriculture in the same year. The disasters are occurring and spreading faster than governments can rebuild. As tens of thousands to hundreds of thousands of lives are upended every year by these "acts of God," the land set apart for the poor in the nations of the world is being transitioned to camps for displaced peoples. There is little reason to suggest these massive populations will escape the classification of displaced peoples in their lifetimes.

In 2017 the late astrophysicist Stephen Hawking warned of the dire need for humans to explore and colonize other planets if our species is to have any hope of survival. Threats from climate change to overpopulation were impossible to ignore, in his estimation. He believed finding new homes on other planets would be our only hope[5]. Two years later, author and geographer Jared Diamond, when discussing his most recent book *Upheaval* about the global crises facing the world, suggested, "I would estimate the chances are about 49 percent that the world as we know it will collapse by about 2050." He added:

> "At the rate we're going now, resources that are essential for complex societies are being managed unsustainably. Fisheries around the world, most fisheries are being managed unsustainably, and they're getting depleted. Farms around the world, most farms are being managed unsustainably. Soil, topsoil around the world. Fresh water

around the world is being managed unsustainably. With all these things, at the rate we're going now, we can carry on with our present unsustainable use for a few decades, and by around 2050 we won't be able to continue it any longer."[6]

A 2015 NASA report found an 80% likelihood of a decades-long megadrought in the American Southwest and Central Plains between 2050 to 2099 based upon soil moisture data sets and climate models[7]. This will upend the American agricultural system. It is vitally important we recognize this is not only an issue of climate change. It is also an issue of mismanagement. The topsoil necessary to grow food is generated over thousands of years. At the current rate of degradation, all the world's topsoil will be gone in 60 years[8].

In 2016, 11% of the world's population, approximately 815 million people, went hungry. By 2050 the global population is expected to grow to 9.8 billion people, creating an increase of 60% on global food demand[9]. The global food system cannot support this. In fact, every current increase on the food system produces compounding effects on food and water supplies around the world. The need for more cows and chickens and wheat places greater demand on water supplies to feed and irrigate these cows and chickens. Those water supplies are already moving into a state of depletion! In 2017 the UN Secretary General warned the global body that the world would begin running out of water by 2050. Demand for water will grow by 40% by that time, and 25% of the world's population will live in countries without access to clean water [10]. Let that sink in for a moment. Twenty-five percent of the world's population will in countries without access to clean water. Who determines who the 25% without access to clean water will be? Wars, genocides and massive human conflicts can be expected to push the losers of such conflicts into the role of those who do not get the drinking water. Included among those wars will be various political arguments, leaders, and doctrines to justify the the atrocities. This is the future we are walking into.

Global conflicts are growing in number and range of violence. The Institute for Economics and Peace reported in its 2018 report there has been an ongoing deterioration of peace, gradual but consistent, over the course of the last decade[11]. As the spread of war and conflict increases, the abundance of armed groups and fighters is growing concurrently. According to a representative from the International Committee of the Red Cross, "We've seen more nonstate armed groups emerge in the last seven years than in the previous 70 years." By the summer of 2018 there were more than 70 non-international conflicts occurring around the world. Fifteen years earlier there were fewer than 30[12]. There is a breaking down of the global order, a fragmenting of the arrangements that have previously held systems together.

These announcements, which we frequently choose to ignore, are the preamble to drastic and overwhelming global crisis that is already beginning to sweep across the world's systems. And these crises are not separate issues but a complex system of cause, effects, and countereffects. The issues of war and conflict are related to the issues of environmental degradation and food and water scarcity. The terror and chaos which this generation is growing all too familiar with is our encounter with the fulfillment of these dark predictions beginning to prove true. We frequently do not recognize what is taking place. Natural disasters or food and water crises are hidden behind political debates and suspicions. Wars and uprisings are "over there" and our daily reality is kept hidden from their effects. But things are shifting around the globe. Things are beginning to fragment and crumble, and unless we are awakened from our numbness and distractions, these crises will overtake us sooner than we realize.

---

1. **Wallace-Wells, David.** The Uninhabitable Earth. *The New York Magazine.* July 10, 2017, Vol. July, July 10, 2017.
2. **Watts, Jonathan.** Biodiversity crisis is about to put humanity at risk, UN scientists to warn. *The Guardian.* [Online] Guardian News & Media Limited, May 3, 2019. [Cited: May 6, 2019.] https://www.theguardian.com/environment/2019/may/03/climate-crisis-is-about-to-put-humanity-at-risk-un-scientists-warn.
3. **Masson-Delmotte, V., P. Zhai, H.-O. Pörtner, D. Roberts, J. Skea, P.R. Shukla, A. Pirani, W. Moufouma-Okia, C. Péan, R. Pidcock, S. Connors, J.B.R.**

Matthews, Y. Chen, X. Zhou, M.I. Gomis, E. Lonnoy, Maycock, M. Tignor, and T. Waterfield (eds.). *IPCC, 2018: Summary for Policymakers. In: Global Warming of 1.5°C. An IPCC Special Report on the impacts of global warming of 1.5°C above pre-industrial levels and related global greenhouse gas emission pathways, in the context of strengthening the global.* Geneva, Switzerland : World Meteorological Organization, 2018.

4. **Fritz, Angela.** The cost of natural disasters this year: $155 billion. *The Washington Post.* [Online] December 26, 2018. [Cited: May 1, 2019.] https://www.washingtonpost.com/weather/2018/12/26/cost-natural-disasters-this-year-billion/?utm_term=.67a09943c79b.

5. **Knapton, Sarah.** Tomorrow's World returns to BBC with startling warning from Stephen Hawking – we must leave Earth. *BBC.* [Online] BBC, May 2, 2017. [Cited: May 1, 2019.] https://www.telegraph.co.uk/science/2017/05/02/tomorrows-world-returns-bbc-startling-warning-stephen-hawking/.

6. **Wallace-Wells, David.** Jared Diamond: There's a 49 Percent Chance the World As We Know It Will End by 2050. *New York Magazine.* [Online] May 10, 2019. [Cited: May 14, 2019.] http://nymag.com/intelligencer/2019/05/jared-diamond-on-his-new-book-upheaval.html.

7. **Steve Cole and Leslie McCarthy.** NASA Study Finds Carbon Emissions Could Dramatically Increase Risk of U.S. Megadroughts. *NASA.GOV.* [Online] NASA, February 2, 2015. [Cited: May 1, 2019.] https://www.nasa.gov/press/2015/february/nasa-study-finds-carbon-emissions-could-dramatically-increase-risk-of-us.

8. **Arsenault, Chris.** Only 60 Years of Farming Left If Soil Degradation Continues. *Scientific American .* [Online] SCIENTIFIC AMERICAN, A DIVISION OF SPRINGER NATURE AMERICA, INC. [Cited: May 6, 2019.] https://www.scientificamerican.com/article/only-60-years-of-farming-left-if-soil-degradation-continues/.

9. **Hincks, Joseph.** The World Is Headed for a Food Security Crisis. Here's How We Can Avert It. *Time.com.* [Online] Time USA, LLC, March 28, 2018. [Cited: May 1, 2019.] http://time.com/5216532/global-food-security-richard-deverell/.

10. **Shaikh, Alanna.** The Bad News? The World Will Begin Running Out of Water By 2050. The Good News? It's Not 2050 Yet. *Un Dispatch.* [Online] June 6, 2017. [Cited: May 1, 2019.] https://www.undispatch.com/bad-news-world-will-begin-running-water-2050-good-news-not-2050-yet/.

11. **http://visionofhumanity.org/.** *Global Peace Index 2018: Measuring Peace in a Complex World.* Sydney, Australia : Institute for Economics & Peace, 2018.

12. **Rosen, Kenneth R.** There's Been a Global Increase in Armed Groups. Can They Be Restrained? *New York Times Magazine.* [Online] June 18, 2018. [Cited: May 1, 2019.] https://www.nytimes.com/2018/06/18/magazine/armed-groups-increase-sudan-icrc.html.

4

MORE THAN CLIMATE CHANGE

Many who read this book will presume I am simply describing the effects of climate change and global warming. I am not. In the course of these pages I contend that what is coming upon our civilization surpasses environmental collapse. (I recognize many believe that to even suggest there is something worse than environmental collapse borders upon heresy.) I deliberately avoid politically charged terms such as climate change, globalization, and many others that might fit in another context. My avoidance of such language is not out of a sense of either denial or presumption. It is a deliberate decision made in the design of this book in hopes of breaking through established mental prejudices. Many readers respond to politicized terminology with either assumptions or denials, both of which I hope to move beyond. These isolated politicized responses are part of what blinds us to the reality of what is actually taking place today. Political language no longer invites cooperation and participation. It invites suspicion and arguments.

If I frame the discussion about population issues around topics of globalization, one group of readers will anticipate a conclusion for greater economic governance and regulation between the haves and the have nots of this world. I might even agree with some of their assumptions, but in these assumptions such readers miss the reality that we have already crossed a threshold in major global issues related to population. Things are much worse than we probably realize. I am not discussing globalization, although many issues addressed in the coming pages might reasonably fall into a category of the effects of globalization. Instead, I am outlining the fundamental systemic collapse within core structures of our global order which has already begun.

Similarly, when I discuss the water crises that are growing wider and more desperate across the planet, many readers will presume I am discussing climate change and environmental issues. Some will immediately tune out at this presumption because they do not trust the hypotheses and prognosticators who are warning of the doom of climate change.

Even in my research for this book, I was surprised at the level of politicization when it came to environmental issues – and this is on both sides. In book after book, I found environmental dangers presented with a frightening urgency only to dissolve into solutions and arguments that are blatantly political and ideological. For example, the book *Extreme Cities - The Peril and Promise of Urban Life in the Age of Climate Change* by Ashley Dawson, describes the growing threats that are already realized across the planet in coastal cities as the ocean's waters rise. Cities like New York and Jakarta are literally sinking into the ocean, and this problem is only going to worsen. By the end of the book, however, Dawson turns to solutions which he classifies as "disaster communism" in order to combat the problems created by "fossil capitalism." How did we move from sinking cities and rising waters to a contest between the 'bad guys' of capitalism and the 'good guys' of communism? The politicization of this disaster might hold elements of fact and truth, but they are lost on readers who approach the topic with doubts to the author's veracity on the subject due to his political objective. This pattern was repeated over and over again in the literature and resources I reviewed for this book when it came to environmental issues.

Politics Are Part of the Problem

Our politicized arguments are part of the problem. They not only suspend any efforts to challenge the disaster that our world is encountering through a polarized gridlock, but they also, literally, make these issues worse. Historically there have been two streams of political response to disaster confronting our world. One argument leans more to the left side of politics and calls for greater central control by the government to empower nations to overcome the challenges. The second argument leans more to the right side of politics and calls for greater freedom in the markets and governments that will allow for innovation and individualism to conquer the growing threats of disaster. Each of these methods has been tried already in a wide range of scales and efforts throughout the world. Each method not only failed but worsened the very problems the society was seeking to defeat. Worse, the historical failures and their societal consequences have reduced trust in the philosophies and governments that are finding themselves impotent to guide societies through the disasters we are now forced to confront.

From the *Great Leap Forward* in China to *The Emergency*[1] in India, strong central government responses of control and management have failed to hold off national disasters in areas such as food scarcity, water resource management, or population control. Strong central government planning made the problems worse, and they destroyed trust in the governing philosophies that inspired them. Likewise, places like Nigeria and South Africa have demonstrated how a free and open market has not led to greater innovation to overcome disaster but rather has isolated wealth to small groups and left the poor to carry the burdens and costs for the society.

This book is not about politics. The end of the world catastrophes which the next half century will unleash are not about politics. While I will take the time to specifically detail the political climate and weaknesses that guarantee the advance and growth of these looming disasters in a later chapter, I will not seek a political solution or identify a political scapegoat for the chaos. There will not be a hidden political ideology creeping behind the facts and various crises that will be explored in the coming chapters.

---

1. For readers who would like to learn more about these events and their consequences, you can access podcast archives on these topics at my web site.

5

PREPPED FOR THE END

Our popular culture is infatuated with the end of the world. Every summer there is a blockbuster movie about the end of the world. The most popular television shows frequently feature the end of the world as a backdrop, usually by way of zombie infestation, alien invasion, or disease outbreak. A popular reality television show today focuses on the plans of doomsday preppers throughout the country and grades their plans on a point system of likely success or failure.

Apocalypse and a fear of the end is something that plays well to the popular imagination in America. D.H. Lawrence once wrote, "Doom! Doom! Doom! Something seems to whisper it in the very dark trees of America. Doom! Doom of what? Doom of our white day." Thoughts about the end of the world have been part of the American identity and consciousness since its founding, usually through apocalyptic religious groups who waited for the end of the world. Those thoughts today have leaped from the domain of religion and doomsday cults to actual political policy in the last two generations. We have been trained and incentivized to think about the end of the world not only by our preachers but by our political leaders and scientists.

A Violent Booming End

There are several popular statistics which note how the 20th century was the bloodiest and deadliest century in the history of the world. More people died by manmade causes in the last century than any century prior. One estimate identifies the total human deaths in the 20th century by war, famine, or government violence against its own citizens at more than 203 million people. The leading cause for this violence was the massive upheaval of World War II. Humanity never experienced anything close to what happened in this historical collision of industrialized and weaponized armies. The flood of death was poured out on both military and civilian targets from Europe to Asia.

Twenty years earlier, the US experienced the deadliest war in its short history when 116,000 Americans were killed during the First World War. In World War II, that death count more than tripled with total American deaths above 405,000. But the US was not even close to the top of the list regarding losses measured by deaths in each nation. That tragic fate belonged to the Soviet Union. More than 24 million Soviet civilians and fighters were killed in World War II! In all, the total dead around the globe after World War II was more than 60 million people. Some even place that number closer to 90 million as the amount of civilian deaths in China during the war was more difficult to track. This is a mind-boggling number and perhaps impossible to comprehend on a personal level. According to legend, the Soviet leader Joseph Stalin, in noting the inability of the human mind to comprehend this scale of death said, "A single death is a tragedy, a million deaths is a statistic."

World War II left the human race traumatized. Civilizations of the old world lay in utter ruins requiring decades to restore. This allowed the United States, which suffered very little in the war relative to its allies and enemies, to ascend in global dominance. But that ascent did not exclude the US from the sense of fear felt by the rest of the world. The people of the world were afraid of what we might unleash upon ourselves next. Throughout the era of the Cold War we believed that if a third World War were to occur it would most certainly mean the end of mankind. We would wipe ourselves out with a nuclear holocaust. The literature and popular media of the 1950s and 1960s are saturated with this fear. Popular television shows like *The Twilight Zone* frequently featured nuclear war and its aftermath among the story themes. Movies like *The Day the Earth Stood Still*, *Dr. Strangelove*, and *Planet of the Apes* betrayed the widespread fear that nuclear war would destroy us all. Popular books like *Alas, Babylon* and *The Long Tomorrow* warned of the destruction our society would most certainly inherit through such an event.

Beyond the popular media, our daily lives were filled with the threat of nuclear war. The children born to the Greatest Generation grew up learning to duck and cover at schools. Bomb shelters were installed in homes among the upper middle class. The Cuban Missile Crisis, unfolding on national television in 1962, brought us to the very brink of global destruction. Special locations were built to withstand a nuclear strike, where members of the different branches of government would be whisked away to, if and when the end arrived. Such locations still exist, along with their plans for use in the event of emergency. Plans were even made for the preservation of our most important documents among the National Archives. The Baby Boomers considered themselves constantly on the brink of the end of the world.

A Degenerating, Choking End

The fall of communism and the end of the Cold War did not bring an end to this fear of the end of the world. Geopolitical concerns were replaced with environmental and climate fears. Most of the world is aware of, but less concerned with, the threat of nuclear war today. Our entertainment, media and politics abound with warnings that we are on the brink of global annihilation because of climate change or global warming.

Simply put, we have been trained to believe the end of the world is coming, and that its arrival is by the hand of man – not God. It was man who made nuclear weapons. It was man who warmed the globe and is melting the polar ice caps. Science and technology have crossed a tipping point! For more than half a century we have been trained to anticipate and fear the end of the world. We may disagree on how the end is going to arrive, but there is an embedded consciousness in our culture that it is certainly coming.

We All Believe in the End of the World

This is not the domain of the lunatic fringe. This is a widespread fear and belief, almost an ethos, sitting below the surface of our day-to-day lives. In March 2017, *The Atlantic* featured an article by Ben Rowan entitled *A Resort for the Apocalypse*[1]. Rowan detailed how the sale and construction of high-end bomb shelters increased by 700% over the prior year. Entire survivalist communities were springing up in remote locations from South Dakota to Germany, funded by the dollars of wealthy tech investors and entrepreneurs. Another report from January of that year by Evan Osnos in the *New Yorker Magazine*[2] cited a survey from *National Geographic* where 40% of Americans believed stocking up on supplies or building a bomb shelter was a smarter investment than a 401k. Survivalism and prepping have taken root among Silicon Valley tech executives and New York hedge fund managers. This new breed of well-funded doomsday preppers is not isolating their fears of the end to just nuclear war or climate change but also to civil unrest brought on by economic inequality, Russian cyberattacks, or natural disasters. Disease pandemics such as an Ebola outbreak also rank high on the list of causes driving their preparations for the end of the world.

End of the world condos have been built in remote areas of Kansas and New Zealand where wealthy clients will fly their families in private jets in the event of the onset of the apocalypse. One tech executive had laser eye surgery performed so as to decrease his level of physical vulnerability in an end of the world situation. These are liberals and conservatives, Republicans and Democrats. The elections of both President Obama and President Trump acted as booms to the end of the world prepper industry. While these super-rich individuals do not brag about how they are prepping for the end of the world, several noted that when the topic comes up among their peers, their steps taken to mitigate personal risks at the end of the world increases their credibility as savvy thinkers and managers of risk.

Fear and anticipation for the end of the world has been programmed into us since World War II. It is a part of our social and psychological DNA. Something is coming. We can sense it! What if these are not the actions of an overly entertained or hyper-paranoid fringe in our society? Could it be that our society's collective subconscious is aware that something is coming? Perhaps all these messages we have been speaking to ourselves for the last half century are simply an internal warning mechanism whose volume is growing louder and louder as it warns us for what lies ahead?

This Time Is Different

...you must understand that in the last days scoffers will come, scoffing and following their own evil desires. They will say, "Where is this 'coming' he promised? Ever since our ancestors died, everything goes on as it has since the beginning of creation."
   2 Peter 3:3,4

Peter warned that scoffers would come at the end of time and mock the idea that the world is ending. Things go on as they always have. In our present context we can interpret this to mean things are bad, but we will find a solution. There is no reason to interpret our modern chaos as the end of the world.

This is one of the most important takeaways I hope readers will gain from this book. The chaos and crisis afflicting the earth today is not the result of bad policies, environmental degradation or even supernatural interference alone. It is all traced back to the state of the human heart. We have more than enough resource and innovation to resolve every crisis being encountered in the earth today. Scarcity of resources or ideas is not what is fracturing the global system. It is the instinctual drives of the human heart toward self-interest that is pushing the chaos forward beyond repair. This instinctual drive of self-interest and others have been present since the beginning of time and human civilization. It is easy to mistake what is occurring today as things that have always occurred since the beginning of creation. The difference today is the full, globalized fruition of the seeds of self-interest in opposition to a God ordained design of cooperation, self-sacrifice, and care for our fellow man. I realize this seems like a pie in the sky perspective at this point. Bear with me. This is much more real than many realize.

The bottom line is this. Things are different today because the fallen human heart is fully expressed in the interconnected global system like never before in history. The whole system reflects the state of the human heart. That is why the system is convulsing. That is why there is chaos as the system begins to collapse. We were not designed, creation was not designed, to operate this way. The only true way to salvage catastrophe is to reshape the nature of the human heart. That of course is a much more daunting task than a new policy or financial aid package.

1. **Rowen, Ben.** A Resort for the Apocalypse. *The Atlantic.* [Online] The Atlantic Monthly, March 2017. [Cited: May 1, 2019.] https://www.theatlantic.com/magazine/archive/2017/03/a-resort-for-the-apocalypse/513869

2. 16. **Osnos, Evan.** Doomsday Prep for the Super Rich . *New Yorker Magazine.* [Online] Conde Nast, January 22, 2017. [Cited: May 1, 2019.] https://www.newyorker.com/magazine/2017/01/30/doomsday-prep-for-the-super-rich.

6

EVERYTHING IS BREAKING

We have been looking in the wrong places for the end. The threats of nuclear holocaust and environmental collapse are significant, but this is not how the end is coming. They could be part of the story, but the true cause of the end of the world, which we will observe over the next half-century, is far less obvious and far more mundane. There will be a widespread fragmenting of the systems of life and order across the world. Instead of a punch to the gut of our global civilization, we will experience a tearing apart at the seams of the very fabric that holds our modern world together. It is a collapse by way of disintegration. And it has already begun!

We see this tearing all around us, even if we do not recognize it. The loss of reason and predictability to explain and define our modern experience is evidence of a tearing apart at the seams of that experience itself; the foundations upon which our civilization is built are collapsing. Imagine a blind man who has walked along the edge of a cliff and suddenly walks off. He does not understand the nature of the chaos he is experiencing. He is still trying to define his experience and reality on the standards and terms present at the edge of the cliff, but his status has changed. He is in freefall. His new status only makes sense when he realizes the loss of security and stability is already in the past. The only thing certain for him now is the inevitable splat that the laws of physics are pulling him toward. His realization and understanding of this new reality will not change the end, but it will reduce his confusion in his present predicament.

So, let's try to understand our current reality. Consider the paradoxes that shape our world today at both an individual and a macro level. Most of the western world, especially the United States, lives in the most prosperous environment the world has ever known. There are several methods to measure wealth, but to keep it simple let us simply measure our modern riches compared to those of former empires on the basis of comfort and ease of living. Imagine the daily work and strain required to manage meals, health, and sanitation -- not to mention the work necessary to prepare for winters when conditions were less conducive for hunting or farming. The modern advent of prosperity and technology has changed all of this, and many of those changes have occurred in less than a century. Those who live as the poor in this country still occupy standards of living that would have been envied by kings and nobles of former empires. From indoor plumbing, air conditioning, cold food, electric stoves, television, and smartphones, the modern family lives a life of luxury and comfort unprecedented in human history. Let us not forget the advances in health, too. In 1900 the average national life expectancy in the United States was 46 years for a man, 48 years for a woman. Today it is 76 and 81 respectively. The length of time we spend enjoying this comfort has nearly doubled in the last century.

Broken Individuals

It is easy to assume that we have achieved some apex of human development due to these advances. That assumption works on paper but not in real life. In real life, our lives are filled with contradictions to the standard of living our civilization has built. In 2019 the World Happiness Report[1] produced by the United Nations Sustainable Solutions Network found that happiness in America has declined for the third year in a row. This was the worst showing for the US in the report's history. The decline in happiness is due to an epidemic of addictions in the US: from gambling to substance abuse, risky sexual behavior to social media usage.

Of course, we don't really need a report from the UN to inform us that Americans are miserable. In 2017, suicide was the tenth leading cause of death. There were 1.4 million attempted suicides that year. Alongside suicide, a massive opioid epidemic is ravaging the country. The number of drug overdose deaths grew by six times the number recorded in 1999. According to the Centers for Disease Control and Prevention, 130 Americans die every day from a drug overdose. Clearly, our living conditions do not align to our living realities. We classify these unnecessary deaths in the most prosperous country in the history of the world as deaths of despair. This is not reasonable. It cannot be defined by logic or rational thought. It is the effect of a society in free fall and collapse.

Broken Homes

As we work our way out from the individual experience and into the wider collective reality, the tearing apart of the binding fabric of humanity effects every facet of human life today. For example, the family is divided and crumbling. In 2014, the Pew Research Center found that fewer than half of American children live in traditional families[2]. The same report demonstrates how 41% of children are now born outside of marriage -- 8 times the rate from fifty years earlier. Recent trends show that the current millennial generation is less interested in marriage. The authority and standard of the family unit declined as this generation grew up in the shadow of diminishing quality of family life. Today, they are asking why they should bother to pursue family. What good is the family unit?

Broken Systems

We have already briefly touched on the divide in our politics, but even our economies are divided. In spite of the significant levels of comfort and luxury we enjoy as individuals, a small minority enjoy much, much more. In 2019, three individuals (Jeff Bezos, Warren Buffett, and Bill Gates) control as much of the nation's wealth as the poorest 50% of Americans, according to inequality.org. The richest 5% of Americans own more than 2/3 of the nation's wealth. This leaves an increasingly smaller and smaller slice of wealth available to the remaining 95% of the country. This is not an indictment on capitalism or cronyism, but simply an observation on how, yet again, divide and separation defines every aspect of our current experience. From race to religion, politics to economics, and the collective national experience to individual wellbeing – division and disintegration has come to define the modern experience. We are coming apart at the seams. We miss this obvious reality only because we keep understanding and interpreting these divisive realities by way of politics and pundits.

This is not only an American phenomenon. The economic inequality that is growing in the United States is scalable to the wider globe. Eight individual rich men own as much of the world's wealth as that distributed to 50% of the world's population - more than 3.75 billion people[3]. When we scale down to the poorest members of these societies where the world's wealth is most thinly distributed, we see further divisions and fragmentations that do not hold up under the burdens of reason and logic.

Broken Nations

A pattern that is growing increasingly frequent across the globe is the irrational and counterproductive distribution of resources. In nations where poverty rages most severely in the forms of food, water, and basic needs for life, a higher percentage of these nations' budgets and resources are not invested in those needs but in weapons and military. The governments are buying more guns and bombs while their people literally starve to death. We can understand this as a cause and effect relationship. Corruption, incompetence, and belligerence are common factors among the leaders of failing states. But this assumption ignores the facts that the global system is feeding this dire situation. The world's leading arms sellers are those nations at the top of the world's wealth ladder. The United States, China, Russia, Germany and France are the top sellers of arms around the world almost every year. Their consumers are the nations where oppression and poverty are a way of life for the people. In other words, the nations which hold the bulk of resources that could alleviate starvation and desperation are leading the way in empowering the authoritarian leaders who propagate the corruption and dysfunction that destroys life among the world's poor.

The various extreme standards of the world, such as rich versus poor, are interacting with one another and promoting further divide, disintegration, and collapse throughout the global system. We can see parallel in almost every facet of society and global order. We are divided and pushing chasm between us wider and wider part. We believe this will keep us stronger and more secure. The reality is we need one another to survive. Division is driving the chaos of our world today.

Normalizing Crisis

There is an old fable that describes how a frog should be boiled. The author of this metaphor has been lost in the retelling through the generations. If one wants to boil a frog, they should not place the frog into a pot of boiling water. The frog will simply jump out after being scalded by the boiling water. Instead, allow the frog to rest in a pot of water at normal temperature. As the frog grows complacent, gradually increase the temperature. Eventually the frog will be lulled to sleep and boiled to death. Unfortunately, our present generation stands in the place of this doomed frog. Every new crisis or catastrophe is a signal that things are growing hotter and the emergency more dire. But we are complacent. We are lulled to sleep. It cannot be all that bad. These situations cannot be related.

We have become too familiar with the term "crisis" to describe events and circumstances afflicting the globe. Economic crisis, terrorism crisis, refugee crisis, political crisis, and the list goes on. Our familiarity with crisis is not simply the result of a sensationalized media but also an increasingly inflamed global predicament. As we investigate deeper into each of these frequent and growing crises, we find the common root of division and disintegration. By understanding this reality, it is easier to more properly identify the so-called crises we are experiencing as symptoms of the truly global crisis of division and disintegration.

Everything is breaking and falling apart. Greater division and disintegration is leading to an escalation of terrorist organizations, activity, and violence. Greater division and disintegration is leading to more internally displaced peoples within nations and more refugees fleeing their homelands. The spread of terrorism, refugees, economic, and political emergencies is not the real crisis. These are the terrible repercussions of a singular underlying and growing fundamental crisis of global divide and disintegration.

Packaged Chaos

In this light, each of these events and circumstances frequently captured in the news headlines could be better understood as packages by which the crisis is being transported across the globe. The refugees fleeing Venezuela, the Sahel, and the Middle East are carrying with them the seeds for contagion, spreading the symptoms of global collapse north, south, east and west. Meanwhile, many fail to notice that terrorist groups today are not focused upon political ends and causes but upon the spread of chaos and destruction beyond the borders of their devastated homelands. Likewise, the political responses of governments and parties meant to resist and oppose these agents spreading the collapse of civilization does nothing to actually slow or halt the crisis but instead amplifies the division and disintegration of the globe. Today every nations of the world finds it necessary to develop a new policy on immigration in the face of the growing refugee crisis. Every nation of the world has a counterterrorism force and policy. The severity and speed of these responses are unique in history, but the displaced person population is still growing. The impact and threat felt by terrorism is still increasing. The more strength exerted by governments to fight the symptoms of crisis, the worse it gets. Such is the state of life in the age of global collapse.

---

1. **Helliwell, J., Layard, R., & Sachs, J.** *World Happiness Report 2019.* New York : Sustainable Development Solutions Network., 2019.
2. **Livingston, Gretchen.** Fewer than half of U.S. kids today live in a 'traditional' family. *Pew Research Center* . [Online] December 22, 2014. [Cited: May 1, 2019.] https://www.pewresearch.org/fact-tank/2014/12/22/less-than-half-of-u-s-kids-today-live-in-a-traditional-family/.
3. **Hardoon, Deborah.** *An Economy for the 99%: It's time to build a human economy that benefits everyone, not just the privileged few* . Oxford : Oxfam, 2017.

PART II

THE SPACE BETWEEN US – THE GLOBAL POPULATION CRISIS

"The parable of our time might well be: Mind your young, or they will trouble you in your old age."
Somini Sengupta

7

GLOBAL CROWDING

I n 2053, the global population is expected to increase by one third, to nearly 10 billion people according to the Population Reference Bureau. This is a number that seemed unimaginable 100 years ago. In 1927, the world's population was at two billion. By 1974, it doubled to four billion. We are expected to reach eight billion in the next couple of years.

Consider the massive events and trends that took place in the past 90 years even as the global population compounded in size. World War II eliminated nearly 3% of the global population. Genocide and ethnic cleansing were hallmarks of dictators who occupied seats of power in much of the world during the second half of the 20th century. If we combine the death counts under Joseph Stalin in the Soviet Union and Mao Zedong in China, more than 65 million people died (a conservative estimate). This death by dictator count does not include Pol Pot, Yahya Khan, or even Hitler. Aggressive family planning, from abortion to birth control, reduced birthrates across the world to such an extent that the world population growth rate peaked in the late 1960s.

But the global population kept growing!

Global population growth is a massive and unstoppable wave that

neither natural disasters, wars, famines, government planning nor
dictators are capable of stopping. As this wave has risen over the
course of the last century, we will see it crash down into widespread
catastrophes by the middle of this century.

LEAST DEVELOPED COUNTRIES IN THE WORLD WHOSE POPULATIONS WILL DOUBLE BY 2050

Angola	Liberia	Zambia
Benin	Madagascar	Afghanistan
Burkina Faso	Malawi	Bangladesh
Burundi	Mali	Bhutan
Central African Republic	Mozambique	Cambodia
Chad	Rwanda	Kiribati
Comoros	Sao Tome and Principe	Lao People's Democratic Republic
Democratic Republic of the Congo	Senegal	Myanmar
Djibouti	Sierra Leone	Haiti
Eritrea	Somalia	Nepal
Ethiopia	South Sudan	Solomon Islands
Gambia	Sudan	Timor-Leste
Guinea	Togo	Tuvalu
Guinea-Bissau	Uganda	Vanuatu
Lesotho	United Republic of Tanzania	Yemen

Forty-eight countries around the world will double in population
size between now and 2050[1]. Sometime around the year 2050, India is
expected to be the most populous country in the world, surpassing
China and growing from a current population of more than 1.3 billion
to nearly 1.8 billion. The nations of Africa are also expected to
demonstrate exceptional growth over the next three decades; the
Democratic Republic of the Congo and Egypt will both be included
in the top ten most populous nations by 2050. The population of the
US is expected to grow by 23 percent in this same time period, one of
the few prosperous industrialized nations that will maintain these
kinds of growth rates. But even with these growth rates the US population will be surpassed by other nations. As Nigeria's population
doubles between now and 2050, it will hold the same population as

the United States by the mid-century mark. The population of the west African nation of Niger will triple by 2050.

Across the globe, birth rates and population counts are swelling. At 280 births per minute, the global population is growing by 403,241 souls a day. Each of these new lives needs food, water, shelter, and hope for a life of opportunity and achievement. Such needs are threatened as resources are not growing at rates proportional to the global population surge. As resources continue to be strained, we will see growing domestic unrest in the nations that are experiencing the greatest threat from this imbalance. The bulging masses of people will push against the fraying edges of other crises such as food and water shortages. Wars, conflicts, and other violence will frequently explode, and the leaders of the world will find it impossible to contain.

This is not a new problem. It is a crisis we have seen coming for decades, even centuries, and yet nothing has been able to stop the impending catastrophe.

---

1. **Westcott, Lucy.** WHAT THE WORLD'S POPULATION WILL LOOK LIKE IN 2050: BY THE NUMBERS. *Newsweek.* [Online] August 25, 2016. [Cited: June 1, 2019.] https://www.newsweek.com/population-growth-2050-asia-africa-europe-493128.

8

A SHORT HISTORY OF POPULATION FEARS

T he study and concern for the rise of human population has a surprisingly robust history. In the closing years of the 18th century, the economist Thomas Malthus wrote what would become his most famous work, An Essay on the Principle of Population. He warned that his generation's population growth rates could not be sustained, and the world was heading toward certain disaster as global population would outstrip global food supplies. Malthus was among the first to point out that global population growth does not merely double or compound from one generation to the next. It grows exponentially.

If we imagine a family tree consisting of one branch for every descendant, a new branch is not added for each generation but for every descendant, thus transforming the family tree into a wildly busy and exploding mass of generations of descendants, which strain the global food supply. This understanding of population growth is significant because, as Malthus pointed out, while population grows exponentially, agriculture does not. Agriculture grows arithmetically. There is a limited amount of farming land, a limited amount of seeds, and a limited amount of livestock that can be produced within the global food supply. When the global population growth meets the limits of that food supply - behold the end is nigh!

Like his intellectual successors in future generations who studied population growth, Malthus was considered a naysayer and a sort of doomsday prophet among contemporary philosophers and economists who were advocating that mankind and the global situation were constantly improving from one generation to the next. His theory was also found to be flawed. While birthrates and population growth could act as significant threats to a limited global food supply, he did not account for unknown future developments in agriculture and food technology. The ability to produce more and more food soon proved to be something that could improve well beyond the arithmetic limitations Malthus foresaw in his own lifetime. As a result, the global population continued to grow and grow - but the end of humanity did not come.

The Population Bomb

Future generations of economists and would-be doomsday prophets encountered the same flaw, and there was a growing legion of critics to their theories about the end of the world. Most significant among these was the American biologist Paul Ehrlich who authored the highly influential 1968 book The Population Bomb. Ehrlich warned that the growth of the human population around the globe was unsustainable and heading toward certain collapse due to limited resources. His warnings came around the same time period that global population growth rates peaked thanks to advances in education and family planning around the world. Ehrlich's predictions may have even helped spur these agendas forward.

GROWTH OF THE GLOBAL POPULATION

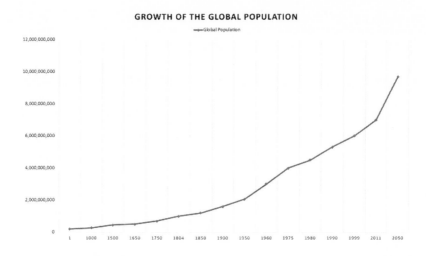

In 1968 global population stood at 3.5 billion, compared to 800 million in 1798 when Malthus published his influential writing. Ehrlich forecasted it would double by 2011. His math was almost perfect. The global population hit 7 billion in 2005. As the population increased rapidly, according to Ehrlich, the global food and resource supply would fail and we would begin to see massive outbreaks of famine, disease, social unrest and the spread of massive global catastrophes.

For some time, the warning issued by Ehrlich was assumed as near fact among study groups at the United Nations, international think tanks, and various non-governmental organizations. Organizations like the Club of Rome and the Sierra Club recommended various policies throughout the international community to reduce the birth rate and limit the growth of the global human population. Frequently, desperately needed financial aid and loans from wealthy nations and organizational patrons to poverty-stricken nations were contingent upon the implementation of population control measures.

While not directly sourced, the fears proposed by The Population Bomb resonated within the social consciousness of the developed world. The 1970s featured a whole genre of science fiction films and literature in which a future dystopian world was ravaged by the strains of overpopulation. Perhaps the most famous of these was

Soylent Green. The 1973 movie starring Charlton Heston (spoiler alert) presented a dire future scenario in which it was revealed that in order to survive, the struggling future human population was being fed recycled and processed human corpses. "Soylent green is people!"

Beyond the social consciousness, however, Ehrlich's warnings resulted in highly controversial policy proposals and, in some instances, implementations. Ehrlich founded the organization Zero Population Growth (later renamed Population Connection) where it was suggested a luxury tax be implemented upon diapers and cribs in more prosperous countries like the United States. The thought was that such a tax would discourage reproduction among young families. In more populous nations plagued with poverty, he advised there should be forced sterilization among all men who had already fathered three children.

Although these policies were not directly implemented, some of the world's largest populated countries did, in fact, establish official measures to reduce population growth and preempt the strain on their future food supply. China implemented its infamous one child policy from 1980 to 2016. Although exceptions could be made, most Chinese citizens were limited to only one child per family. Violators of the policy faced harsh financial repercussions, or worse. Over the timespan of the policy, more than 324 million Chinese women were fitted with intrauterine devices and 107 million were sterilized.

In 1975, India sterilized 6.2 million of its male citizens, focusing specifically upon the poor. Critics since this time have noted that this was 15 times more than what the Nazis sterilized in their concentration camps during World War II. As recently as 2013 to 2014, India carried out over 4 million sterilizations; more than 95% of these were surgically performed upon women[1].

In spite of these harsh policies and decisions to confront the dark realities proposed in books like The Population Bomb one stubborn and irrefutable fact remains. The global population has continued to grow as forewarned – but the end has not come.

Like Thomas Malthus over 200 years ago, critics to Paul Ehrlich and The Population Bomb argue that the warnings of global collapse

due to human population outstripping the global food supply failed
to properly account for changes in agricultural technology. Human
ingenuity is a more powerful factor than we realized and likely saved
the world from Ehrlich's dire predictions.

---

1. **Biswas, Soutik.** India's dark history of sterilisation. *BBC.* [Online] BBC News,
November 14, 2014. [Cited: June 1, 2019.] http://www.bbc.com/news/world-asia-
india-30040790.

9

WE HAVE BEEN LOOKING AT THE WRONG NUMBERS

Were global population prophets of doom like Ehrlich and Malthus wrong? The answer is no. They were simply looking at the wrong numbers. Even while global population has continued to increase and the food supply has continued to grow (we will look at food and water crises in parts three and four of this book), other trends have developed which neither Malthus nor Ehrlich predicted - but perhaps they should have.

A growing disparity exists between the most prosperous nations of the world and the most poverty stricken. The gap between the wealthy nations and poor nations is growing incredibly fast. This is a trend that has accelerated since World War II. Corresponding to this growth, new trends in the global population distribution have been left almost completely unnoticed by the academic and government bodies around the world.

**20 YOUNGEST NATIONS IN THE WORLD
AND THEIR GDP PER CAPITA**

COUNTRY	MEDIAN AGE	GDP PER CAPITA
NIGER	15.4	$378
MALI	15.8	$824
UGANDA	15.8	$604
ANGOLA	15.9	$4,170
MALAWI	16.5	$338
ZAMBIA	16.8	$1509
BURUNDI	17	$320
MOZAMBIQUE	17.2	$415
BURKINA FASO	17.3	$670
SOUTH SUDAN	17.3	$237
TANZANIA	17.7	$936
LIBERIA	17.8	$456
CHAD	17.8	$669
ETHIOPIA	17.9	$767
SOMALIA	18.1	$499
BENIN	18.2	$829
NIGERIA	18.4	$1,968
SAO TOME AND PRINCIPE	18.4	$1,912
CAMEROON	18.5	$1,446
GABON	18.6	$7,220

Comparison:

COUNTRY	MEDIAN AGE	GDP PER CAPITA
USA	36.8	$59,531
EU	42.6	$38,500
JAPAN	46.9	$38,428

The problem is not a global population boom. It is a youth population bulge. The fastest growing countries in the world also feature the youngest and poorest populations of the world. The young are growing desperate and angry.

Note: 1 GDP per capita is a country's total annual GDP divided by the total population count. It is an important economic measurement for recognizing living standards and well-being.

Population and birth rates in developed nations, generally in the west, have trended in the opposite direction warned of by Ehrlich. Meanwhile, population growth in less developed nations has outperformed the forecasts. As a result, not only are the rich nations getting richer and the poor nations getting poorer, but the rich are growing fewer and the poor are growing more numerous.

In 2015 the United States had its lowest rate of population growth at any time since the end of the Great Depression[1]. This was due largely to the fact that more people were dying of old age than were being born. In 2015, more people died in the US than in any year since 2000. This was not due to a great national tragedy or crisis but the simple aging of the population. The Greatest Generation and the Baby Boomers are dying of old age. The difference between this moment and the similar statistical events of prior generations is that these aging members of America's population are not being replaced by new births or young immigrants.

In the developed world, the birth rate has dropped below the "replacement rate" of 2.1 children per woman in her lifetime. It now sits at 1.86 in the United States[2]. Meanwhile, the global population continues to grow. A United Nations reports suggests the 2015 global population of approximately 7.3 billion people will reach somewhere between 9.6 billion to 12.3 billion by the end of this century. This growth is obviously not coming from the developed world. It is coming from the underdeveloped world where poverty and corruption are leading to increasing political and military unrest.

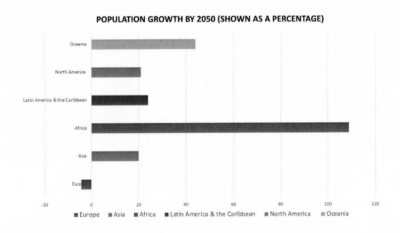

POPULATION GROWTH BY 2050 (SHOWN AS A PERCENTAGE)

Regional population growth around the world by 2050

Consider the implications of this demographic shift in America and keep in mind these trends are even more pronounced in Europe. As the population ages and is not consistently replaced by younger members in the work force, a growing burden of care for the aging population is placed upon fewer and fewer working members. This is part of the cause of the strain upon the middle class in the modern American economy. Fewer young members of the American work-force are available to fund programs such as Social Security, Medicare, or long term care needs for the generation that includes their parents and grandparents. This leads to greater stretching of the nation's financial resources among the working middle class, greater resentment, and philosophical political shifts.

Ironically, the one people group that could relieve this burden placed on the thinning middle class -- immigrants -- is presented as yet another burden to the younger generation. America has always struggled with class warfare when it comes to immigration, but in the long-term immigrants provide a vital stability for countries with aging populations. Today an inflow of immigrants could help to both financially support and replace America's aging generation. Instead, the dominating narrative is that immigration means more poor people living off of the middle-class tax dollar. There is some level of truth to this accusation, but it is not the whole truth.

The greater threat actually lies beyond the borders of America, within the developed world. It comes via the shifting population demographics of the poorer nations of the earth. As Somini Sengupta expressed in a 2016 New York Times editorial:

> "At no point in recorded history has our world been so demographically lopsided, with old people concentrated in rich countries and the young in not-so-rich countries. Much has been made of the challenges of aging societies. But it's the youth bulge that stands to put greater pressure on the global economy, sow political unrest, spur mass migration and have profound consequences for everything from marriage to Internet access to the growth of cities." [3]

At the time of Sengupta's article, a quarter of all humans alive on planet earth were between the ages of 10 and 24. As we have already seen, they are not living in the prosperous developed world. The United Nations Population Fund confirms that the vast majority of these young people live in the developing world.

TOP 10 LARGEST CITIES IN THE WORLD	POPULATION	NATIONAL MEDIAN AGE
KARACHI, PAKISTAN	17.1 million	22
DHAKA, BANGLADESH	18.2 million	26
CAIRO EGYPT	19.1 million	23
OSAKA, JAPAN	20.3 million	47
MEXICO CITY, MEXICO	21.2 million	28
BEIJING, CHINA	21.2 million	37
SÃO PAULO, BRAZIL	21.2 million	32
MUMBAI, INDIA	23.3 million	29
SHANGHAI, CHINA	24.4 million	37
DELHI, INDIA	26.4 million	29

This young population has grown up in the shadow of western prosperity and values. While it may not have been packaged as "The American Dream," the sentiments exported throughout the world through satellite television and the internet were much the same. Work hard. Go to school. Obey the rules. Get a good job and your life will be better than that of your parents. To that end, more of these young people were educated, informed, and exposed to western values and promises than those of prior generations. The underdeveloped world has seen a swelling of the ranks of their young people entering the education system in recent decades, from primary school to universities.

Unfortunately, as these young people exited college and entered the workforce they found the promises they worked for were not waiting for them. Corrupt and incompetent leaders have not fostered economic growth policies, even while they promoted the education of their youth. Infrastructure has not been altered to receive this booming youth population. Resource distribution is not equipped to sustain them. Education alone does not result in a prosperous economy!

This context and reality of the global population should change the way we understand many of the modern issues and events unfolding around us. The Arab Spring in the Middle East and North Africa in 2012 was not about the rise of democracy, as much of the more prosperous world was led to believe. To the youth population bulge, it was about jobs and the perception of broken promises.

---

1. **Bahrampour, Tara.** U.S. population growth is lower than at any time since the Great Depression. *The Washington Post.* [Online] December 22, 2016. [Cited: January 3, 2018.] https://www.washingtonpost.com/local/social-issues/us-population-growth-is-lower-than-at-any-time-since-the-great-depression/2016/12/21/5267e480-c7ae-11e6-85b5-76616a33048d_story.html?utm_term=.7c02a767c9f6.

2. **Gao, George.** Scientists more worried than public about world's growing population. *Pew Research Center.* [Online] June 8, 2015. [Cited: June 1, 2019.] http://www.pewresearch.org/fact-tank/2015/06/08/scientists-more-worried-than-public-about-worlds-growing-population/.

3. **Sengupta, Somini.** Opinion | The World Has a Problem: Too Many Young People. *New York Times.* [Online] New York Times, March 5, 2016. [Cited: June 1, 2019.] https://www.nytimes.com/2016/03/06/sunday-review/the-world-has-a-problem-too-many-young-people.html

10

THE POPULATION PROBLEM IN EGYPT –
A CASE STUDY

T o understand the impact and nature of the population issue in the developing world, it is helpful to study a particular country in order to see the threads of unrest and ultimately disaster running throughout its history. Similar facts and realities present in Egypt can be seen in many of the fastest growing countries throughout the world.

It is important to note that Egypt has been continuously ruled by a military figure since the overthrow of the monarchy in 1952. The Arab Spring in 2011 produced a short break from military rule when democratic elections placed a member of the Muslim Brotherhood into power. Mohamed Morsi ruled from June 30, 2012 to July 3, 2013. He was then ousted from power in a military coup. Today, General Abdel Fattah el-Sisi, a former Egyptian military member, rules the country. In most contexts we would recognize more than half a century of military rule as a military dictatorship.

Additionally, in recent decades Egyptian life under military rule have been decades of increasing economic and political dysfunction. Central to that economic dysfunction is a booming population and widening gap between the powerful rich minority and the growing masses of poor Egyptians. As the consequences of these dysfunctions began to manifest, the authoritarian hand of Egypt's military rulers became more and more apparent.

Since the end of the Egyptian monarchy after World War 2, one of the most daunting issues confronting Egypt is its population explosion. In the 100 years after 1880, Egypt's population grew by more than 600%. The 1947 census recorded an Egyptian population of nearly 19 million people. By 1976 that number had almost doubled to 36.6 million. A mere 10 years later, in 1986, the Egyptian population stood at 50.4 million. It has been growing ever since.

Egypt's economic and agricultural systems were not equipped to support this level of growth. Many Egyptians began leaving their country, working abroad and sending their paychecks home to family members. Anwar Sadat, in order to court influence from the United States and western democracies, began to liberalize the Egyptian economy when he came to power in the 1970s. His aggressive free market policies allowed for a sudden surge in the gap between the haves and the have-nots in the country. Egypt's rich and powerful became much more rich and powerful while the poor became much poorer, and also more numerous. During the late 1970s, while much of the world was focused on the Camp David Accords US President Jimmy Carter was mediating between Sadat and Israeli Prime Minister Begin, the priorities were starkly different in Egypt. In January of 1977, *"Bread Riots"* broke out in the major cities of Egypt as food prices exploded by 50%. Hundreds of thousands of protests erupted across the country. These protesters were frustrated by austerity measures enforced upon them by Sadat's government, working in line with the World Bank and International Monetary Fund[1]. Sadat deployed the military to put down the riots. At least 70 people were killed, with hundreds more injured. One year later on the anniversary of the *Bread Riots,* the President of the World Bank declared that Egypt could expect no more support from the organization until its population growth was brought under control. The real issue behind Egypt's economic dysfunction at the end of the 1970s, according to the experts, was population control.[2]

The population growth has not stalled and neither has the worsening of Egypt's economic dysfunctions since that time. The conditions that were beginning to come to fruition under Sadat only increased under Hosni Mubarak's military rule. At the outset of the Arab Spring in 2010, life satisfaction among the middle class of Egypt was among the lowest in the world. Egyptians were frustrated and dissatisfied with their government, public transportation, quality healthcare and quality of jobs. By 2008 the population of Egypt had grown to 82 million, and people were increasingly fed up with the standard of life and failed promises made to them by the Mubarak government. The demographics of this expanded population are even more telling. More than 60% of Egypt's population was under the age of 30. Forty percent of the people were between the ages of 10 and 29. Food prices were continuing to rise, employment prospects were dim, and the promises of access and opportunity made to them by the democratic institutions of the world like the World Bank had failed. By 2010 Egypt was at the apex of the youth population bulge.

Arab Spring captivated the world's attention as protesters filled Tahrir Square in Egypt, but the root issues did not change. Mubarak was removed from power, and today a new military general sits atop the Egyptian political hierarchy, but headlines from the past two years in Egypt are remarkably similar to those of the Sadat years in the late 1970s. In the summer of 2018, economic reforms imposed upon Egypt by the International Monetary Fund were taking a significant toll on the average Egyptian. Fuel prices were up 50% [3]. Youth unemployment was above 30%. Electricity prices for manufacturers rose by 41%, and 20% for households. These increased by another 15% one year later in the summer of 2019. The price of drinking water was up by 50% [4]. It is easy allow our minds to grow numb when reading over such statistics. But imagine the impact to your home, family and life ambitions if the price of fuel, unemployment, electricity and drinking water were to increase in this manner. These sort of economic hits drastically shake social and economic stability.

Austerity measures have not worked in Egypt. Since the 1970s, the impositions from the World Bank and the International Monetary Fund have taken a heavy toll upon the people of Egypt but have not changed the economic realities in this country. Foreign aid from the US and international community likewise have not alleviated Egypt's struggles and cannot be seen as means to the real solution. Similarly, incompetence and corruption within the government are significant issues afflicting Egypt. But none of these issues are the real problem. The real problem is one of population.

Egypt holds one of Africa's fastest growing national populations at 93 million people at the time of this writing. Economic and political reforms cannot keep up with this birthrate and neither can the natural resources. The effects of the 2008 global food crisis (we will look at this in part 3) were largely centered upon Egypt. That unique crisis was brought about by more than population growth, but the incredible growth of Egypt's population helped emphasize the struggles of the food crisis within that country. The Nile River is being sucked dry. Each person in Egypt uses 160,000 gallons of water per year. That figure will be forced to drop to 130,000 gallons by 2030 due to Egypt's population growth alone[5]. This barely accounts competition for the Nile's waters by Ethiopia at Egypt's southern border. Between 2010 to 2012, the youth unemployment rate in Egypt surged from 26.3% to 38.3%[6]. The Egyptian economy did not have enough jobs to satisfy its ever-growing population.

The fear of food and water scarcity were among the causes for a massive awareness campaign launched in the 1980s and continuing over the course of several decades aimed at reducing the birth rate in Egypt. Contraception was made available to the poor. Public service announcements were placed on billboards in poor and rural areas. To some extent these efforts were successful, but only temporarily. By the time of the 2011 revolution, the growth rate was rising again. It continued to climb after the toppling of Hosni Mubarak[7]. Between the lines of these statistics we can see the human psychology at work. The youth of Egypt saw their problems centered upon Mubarak, and once he was gone, they were going to be all right, and their problems would resolve. Therefore, having sex and continuing to grow the population was practically part of the revolution.

Unfortunately, the removal of Mubarak did not solve the nation's problems, and the growing birth rate and population only added to the strain upon the country. Since the Arab Spring and its demise, terrorism has increased in Egypt. This increase of terrorist activity has been the justification for numerous policies by the Egyptian military government, including a state of emergency enacted at the end of 2017 and maintained to the present. Terrorism is difficult to define in an academic sense, but it is a useful means for the governments of strained nations to suppress dissent. Between 2013 and 2017, 60,000 people were imprisoned in Egypt, most of these as political prisoners. Ten new prisons were built. Military courts were established to prosecute civilians. Extra judicial killings, torture, and "forced disappearances" are frequently reported in Egypt by various human rights organizations. New laws and policies to silence the media were also enacted in 2017 [8].

Youth migration from Egypt to Europe has increased dramatically. According to a 2016 report from the International Organization for Migration: Since 2011, the percentage of unaccompanied children among Egyptian irregular migrants reaching Europe has been remarkably high. In 2014, they accounted for nearly half of 4,095 irregular Egyptian migrants arriving in Italy. In 2015, Italy registered the arrival of some 1,711 Egyptian children – more than from any other country[9].

The most important aspect of the observations regarding the trends and dysfunctions in Egypt is that they are all rooted to uncontrollable population growth. These trends can be replicated across the globe in a growing number of nations who have seen their populations explode over the course of the last half century and who are expected to see the same trends continue in the coming decades. Like Egypt, as these nations see population explosions, there will be, and indeed have already begun to be, repercussions across their economies and political environments. In many places where we see growing terrorism, refugee crises, civil unrest, coups, war, political instability as well as food, water, and resource shortages, we will find population explosions sitting at the root. This was forecast in the 1960s. Today it is not a forecast. It is a reality that helps explain the chaos of the world all around us. If we want to understand the chaos of the world all around us, we have to understand the youth population bulge sitting at the root of it.

---

1. The World Bank is a feature of the post-World War 2 global economy. Its purported goals are to assist emerging markets to reduce extreme poverty. The second goal of the organization is to increase the share of prosperity. It is an international organization in which the United States has a controlling voting interest.

    The International Monetary Fund (IMF) is another post-World War 2 feature of the global economy. Founded upon the principles of capitalism and free markets, the IMF works "to foster global monetary cooperation, secure financial stability, facilitate international trade, promote high employment and sustainable economic growth, and reduce poverty around the world."

2. *Excecutive Intelligence Review.* **Dreyfuss, Bob.** 4, New York : Campaigner Publications, 1978, Vol. 5.

3. **Magdy, Samy.** Egypt increases fuel prices, as part of austerity measures . *Associated Press.* [Online] June 16, 2018. [Cited: June 1, 2019.] https://www.apnews.com/1c19c3641d82477ab110948ece554845.

4. **Ahmed, Sarah.** Drinking Water Prices Increase Nearly 50% in Egypt. *Egyptian Streets.* [Online] Egyptian Streets, June 3, 2018. [Cited: June 1, 2019.] https://egyptianstreets.com/2018/06/03/drinking-water-prices-increase-nearly-50-in-egypt/.

5. **SCHWARTZSTEIN, PETER.** FORGET ISIS, EGYPT'S POPULATION BOOM IS ITS BIGGEST THREAT. *Newsweek.* [Online] Newsweek, March 20, 2017. [Cited: January 6, 2018.] http://www.newsweek.com/2017/03/31/egypt-population-birth-rate-food-water-shortage-isis-terrorism-sissi-570953.html.

6. **SABHA, ASSIN.** Youth Employment in Egypt and Tunisia vs. Jordan and Morocco Three Years After the Arab Awakening. *The World Bank Voices and Views the Middle East and North Africa.* [Online] The World Bank, April 18, 2014. [Cited: January 6, 2018.] http://blogs.worldbank.org/arabvoices/youth-employment-egypt-and-tunisia-vs-jordan-and-morocco-three-years-after-arab-awakening.

7. **SCHWARTZSTEIN, PETER.** FORGET ISIS, EGYPT'S POPULATION BOOM IS ITS BIGGEST THREAT. *Newsweek.* [Online] Newsweek, March 20, 2017. [Cited: January 6, 2018.] http://www.newsweek.com/2017/03/31/egypt-population-birth-rate-food-water-shortage-isis-terrorism-sissi-570953.html.

8. **Al Jazeera News.** Egypt's Emergency Law Explained. *Al Jazeera News.* [Online] April 11, 2017. [Cited: January 6, 2018.] http://www.aljazeera.com/indepth/features/2017/04/egypt-emergency-law-explained-170410093859268.html.

9. **Feller, Nils.** *Egyptian Unaccompanied Migrant Children: A case study on irregular migration.* Cairo, Egypt : International Organization for Migration, 2016.

11

POPULATION CLUSTER BOMBS

W hen we see the underlying issues of politics and economics taking shape in nations around the world, we interpret events like the Arab Spring differently. It's clear these underlying issues are built upon nearly immovable disasters such as population explosions and food and water shortages, therefore events like the Arab Spring, coups, and other dramatic actions should be recognized as inevitable. The rising number of civil wars, terrorist groups, and protests throughout the world are not about a desire for western values and democracy. They are about a fed up and frustrated mass of youth. They have come to realize that the world is not going to be better in their lifetime. In fact, it is going to be worse! There is less space, fewer resources, less food, less water, and fewer opportunities than ever before. The rich are getting richer, the poor are getting poorer, and the rich are getting fewer while the poor are growing more numerous.

We should not pretend that all of the unrest and upheaval is coming from poor or impoverished people. The rich nations will, and already are, taking steps to prevent the contagion of chaos from areas like North Africa, the Middle East, and other parts of the world from spreading to their borders. The coming decades will see a growing trend of hardline policies, political parties, and initiatives aimed to protect the world's haves from the chaos spreading out from the have-nots. Today the more prosperous nations of the northern hemisphere label these politics and rhetoric as nationalism, but by 2025 it will be much more en vogue and politically correct.

Paul Ehrlich foresaw a global population bomb. In fact, it is not a global population bomb but a population cluster bomb being set off in various pockets and corners of the globe simultaneously, exploding with exponential rates of impact from Asia to Africa. It has already begun!

According to the Population Reference Bureau[1], most of the globe's population growth in the coming decades will take place in Africa, Asia and Latin America. Latin America's growth rates will remain largely constant, but Asia will grow faster as the growth in Europe and the United States declines. Leading the club of population growth will be the continent of Africa.

- Nigeria, currently the seventh most populous country in the world, is expected to overtake the United States by 2050 and be among the top five most populous countries in the world.
- The Democratic Republic of Congo had a population of 79.8 million in 2017, but that is expected to grow to 214 million by 2050 thanks to a fertility rate of 4.53 births per woman.
- Ethiopia experienced an annual population growth of 2.5% between 2010 and 2015. As the second most populous nation on the African continent, it is expected to grow from 101 million people to 168.6 million by 2050.
- Tanzania is expected to nearly triple in size between 2015 and 2050, from 54.2 million people to 134.8 million. The nation's capital Dar es Salaam anticipates 85% growth between 2016 and 2025 – a span of nine years!
- Uganda has the fastest growing population in the world. Its national population will grow from 36.6 million to 101.5

million by 2050. The capital Kampala will grow from 6
million to 20 million between 2013 and 2040[2].

Much of North Africa, including Tunisia, Egypt, Morocco, and
Algiers are also expected to be sites of leading population growth in
the next 30 years. In the best of situations, this places these locales as
ideal spots for investment for future growth, but it also makes them
potential hotbeds for political instability. It is worth noting and care-
fully considering how these North African nations have been
frequently featured in the news of the last half-decade for everything
from Arab Spring, rising terrorist attacks, coups, human trafficking,
and as ports of exit for refugees disembarking for Europe.

While African nations are leading the way in population growth
over the next 45 years, they are not alone. Also among the top ten
fastest growing nations are India, which is expected to grow by 467
million by 2050, Pakistan by 101 million, and the Philippines by 62
million.

All of these nations, and those that missed the top of the population growth lists but are still far outpacing the developed world, share
many characteristics. Improving healthcare has greatly assisted in
this population growth. This has resulted in lower mortality rates and
higher fertility rates. A cultural value for large families and social
acceptance for early motherhood is also a common thread. Many of
the nations also share the same religion. Globally, Islam has the
highest birth rate, with Christianity second. A recent study by the
Pew Research Center suggests that by the year 2050, Islam will
replace Christianity as the world's largest religion due to the rapid
growth of Muslim populations.

"While the world's population is projected to grow 32% in the
coming decades, the number of Muslims is expected to increase by
70% – from 1.8 billion in 2015 to nearly 3 billion in 2060. In 2015,
Muslims made up 24.1% of the global population. Forty-five years
later, they are expected to make up more than three-in-ten of the
world's people (31.1%). The main reasons for Islam's growth

ultimately involve simple demographics. To begin with, Muslims have more children than members of the seven other major religious groups analyzed in the study. Muslim women have an average of 2.9 children, significantly above the next-highest group (Christians at 2.6) and the average of all non-Muslims (2.2). In all major regions where there is a sizable Muslim population, Muslim fertility exceeds non-Muslim fertility." **Pew Research Center**[3]

Even in those rapidly growing nations where Islam is not the majority religion, there is cause for other concerns as the belief systems within many of such nations are split. For example, in India the percentage of the population who adheres to traditional Hindu beliefs recently dropped below 80% while the growth of the Muslim minority has increased annually. The formation of India as a distinct entity from Pakistan was built upon a division between Hindu and Muslim populations on the subcontinent. Extremist groups on both the Hindu and Muslim sides of the religious divide are frequently responsible for inflaming situations in the most poverty-stricken areas of the country. When we dig deeper into the violence and the conflicts however, we find the real grievances are the results of resource scarcity as growing populations stretch the nations' supplies beyond exhaustion. Religious ideology is simply allowing the violence to be morally acceptable among these groups.

We see such tensions demonstrated in Nigeria. In April 2014, the terrorist organization Boko Haram was featured in the global media lens when they claimed responsibility for the kidnapping of more than 275 teenage girls from the government sponsored secondary school in Chibok, Nigeria. The outrageous action prompted the social media movement #BringBackOurGirls and gained Boko Haram infamy. The story of the Chibok girls is only the tip of the iceberg to Boko Haram's atrocities. Bombings, rape, suicide attacks, beheadings using chainsaws, and death counts that range in the tens of thousands make Boko Haram one of the most deadly, violent, and horrific terrorist groups of the 21st century - so far. But to understand the forces behind the ascension of Boko Haram in Nigeria, the true story does not begin with terrorism.

Nigeria is among the most populous nations on the African continent. It also hosts the most prosperous economy, its chief export being oil. Cocoa is the second largest export for Nigeria, but makes up only 0.7% of Nigeria's exports. Thus, the Nigerian economy is largely dependent upon oil consumers in the developed world. Nigeria is also a nation that could be split into pieces between various religions and ethnic groups. The north contains the bulk of Nigeria's Muslim population, which account for 50% of all Nigerians while another 40%, largely based in the southern part of the country, profess Christianity. The oil and natural gas wealth is situated largely in the Christian, southern region of the nation. The further north one travels in Nigeria, the more likely they are to encounter Muslims and poverty.

At the most northeastern point of a map of Nigeria, we find a region known as Borno State. Here per-capita income is 50% less in than what is found in the south. Borno has a literacy rate two-thirds lower than that of Nigeria's capital city Lagos which is located in the Christian south. Less than 5% of women can read or write in Borno. Although Nigeria as a whole boasts a high birth rate, in 2013 the 5.5 birth rate of the nation was contrasted against the 6.3 birth rate in the northeast. Unemployment and poverty are also at their highest extremes there. The causes for Borno's appalling dysfunction relative to the Christian south in Nigeria is related largely to government incompetence and corruption. According to Transparency International in 2013, 9 out of 10 Nigerians said the police were corrupt and 45% said the military was corrupt. Former President Sani Abacha is alleged to have stolen over $1.1 billion from the country. The same organization's annual Government Defense Anti-Corruption Index, which ranked 82 countries according to corruption, showed Nigeria in the top tier of nations with a high corruption risk. Newly elected Nigerian President Buhari has reported that in the last decade over $150 billion has been stolen from the country by corrupt government officials and administrators. Upon taking office, Buhari implemented a $2.1 billion intervention package to help bankrupt Nigerian states pay owed salaries to government workers. At least 12 of Nigeria's 36 states were said to back-owe more than $550 million in salaries, with many employees having been unpaid for as long as seven months.

This is the state of affairs in one of the fastest growing nations in the world. As oil wealth accelerated, so did the disparity between northern and southern Nigeria. Accompanying this disparity was a rapid growth in corruption among the powerful and wealthy classes, dominated predominantly by the powerful Christian southern part of the nation. As a result, unemployment grew in the north, and so did poverty and failing education rates. The one thing that did not decrease was the birth rate. More people are being born in the north than in the south, straining already tense communities and family budgets. Nigeria was simply waiting for the proverbial spark to light this powder keg and push a massive population of unemployed, desperate, frustrated and growing numbers of unemployed young men into extremism. That spark came in the crash of the oil markets in 2014. Boko Haram predated the oil crash, but their ranks swelled and the extremism blossomed afterward. The price of oil fell from between $100 and $125 a barrel to $40. That translated to a terrible catastrophe for Nigeria's economy.

Today the threat and activity of Boko Haram is one of the primary threats to the Nigerian state, even while the government continues to struggle with issues of economy, corruption, and continuing down-turns in the oil market. Boko Haram's threat has spread to neighboring countries and caused a regional increase in anti-terrorism and guerilla activity. The organization itself is now morphing and even faces new competitors in the Borno region and beyond. Local populations remain terrorized by both Boko Haram and the Nigerian government's hard line response to the militants.

The story of Boko Haram is a story that is becoming a dominant thread in the global narrative throughout the developing world. From India to Pakistan to Somalia to the Philippines, where population rates are surging, we also see poverty and corruption coinciding.

These forces give rise to desperation and extremism among the local population. These responses do not yield a solution but simply a kicking back against the powers that be. In that kicking back, a sort of contagion effect takes hold so that the threat of these terrorist groups spreads across neighboring borders in the form of direct attacks or refugee crises from people fleeing from the terrorist organizations.

---

1. **Population Reference Bureau.** World Population Growth, 1950–2050. *Population Reference Bureau.* [Online] Population Reference Bureau. [Cited: January 5, 2018.] http://www.prb.org/Publications/Lesson-Plans/ HumanPopulation/PopulationGrowth.aspx.
2. **Adegoke, Yemisi.** UN: Half of world's population growth is likely to occur in Africa. *CNN.* [Online] CNN, June 25, 2017. [Cited: January 6, 2018.] http://www. cnn.com/2017/06/25/africa/africa-population-growth-un/index.html.
3. **Hackett, Michael Lipka and Conrad.** Why Muslims are the world's fastest-growing religious group. *Pew Research Center.* [Online] Pew Research Center, April 6, 2017. [Cited: January 6, 2018.] http://www.pewresearch.org/fact-tank/2017/ 04/06/why-muslims-are-the-worlds-fastest-growing-religious-group/.

12

THIS IS ONLY THE BEGINNING

Throughout the world we have young populations looking through the windows of an interconnected global landscape and seeing smaller, older populations holding a monopoly on the majority of the world's wealth. It is not difficult for extremists and religious ideologues to convert this frustration and disenfranchisement to hostile and violent action. The detonation of these cluster bombs will spread from "over there" to "right here."

In fact, it has already begun! In the middle of this current decade, Europe found itself experiencing a massive refugee crisis. More than 300,000 refugees risked their lives crossing the Mediterranean to find refuge on European soil. This refugee crisis reshaped European politics, igniting a surge of nationalism and nationalist candidates in many southern European countries and a recalibration of human rights and values across the political landscape of the continent. While the refugees were fleeing for their lives from war-torn homelands, more sinister elements embedded themselves among the refugees. Several ISIS terrorist attacks within Europe came from attackers who reached their targets while posing as refugees. This violence was leveraged to justify an intensification of nationalist rhetoric and escalated fear and priorities for national security in both Europe and the US. In the European and western democratic societies least impacted by the effects of youth population explosions and resource scarcity, walls are going up to stop the spread of the chaos. These walls are both literal and figurative. Recognizing these realities reshapes the way we interpret domestic and global politics.

But the incredible part is that the refugee crisis that fueled so much political transformation across Europe was only a fringe effect of the greater crisis taking shape in other parts of the world. No nation of Europe was even among the top ten nations most heavily impacted by refugees since 2010 – not even at the height of the refugee crisis.

1. Jordan 2.7 million +
2. Turkey 2.5 million +
3. Pakistan 1.6 million +
4. Lebanon 1.5 million +
5. Iran 979,400
6. Ethiopia 736,100
7. Kenya 553,900
8. Uganda 477,200
9. Democratic Republic of the Congo 383,100
10. Chad 369,500

Top 10 Nations Receiving Refugees in 2016

The refugee crisis is directly related to the youth population bulge taking shape in the developing world. Note the proximity of terrorist attacks (the chart below) to the spread of refugees from this crisis.

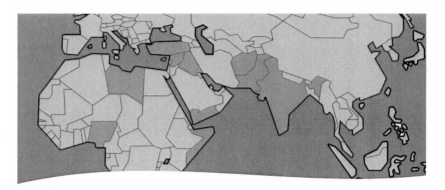

Nations Experiencing Most Frequent Terrorist Attacks

1. Iraq
2. Afghanistan
3. Nigeria
4. Syria
5. Pakistan
6. Yemen
7. Somalia
8. India
9. Turkey
10. Libya

The United States is leading the way in the war on terrorism, but the bulk of the world's terrorist attacks are nowhere near the US or US interests. This war, arguably an overreaction, is a response to the contagion effect of deeper crises. As the more prosperous nations of the world intensify their hardline stances and reduce assistance to the underdeveloped world, the crisis will worsen and the chaos will spread. Victims of the nations hardest hit by the chaos will justify their own insurgent responses toward the nations of prosperity. A certain cycle of predictability and intensification will result. The violence from the carriers of the chaos inspires greater and harder measures for security from the prosperous nations, which feeds the narratives that produce more carriers of chaos. The coming decades will be defined by a growing contagion of the chaos even while our views and experience within this global reality become more polarized. To understand the growing chaos of the world around us we do not need to examine terrorism or refugee crises. We must go deeper to the foundational issues that are driving the chaos.

Population growth is merely one of the foundational elements of global order that is crumbling. In part three we will look at the next foundational element that is also crumbling, the global food system. This crisis is intensified by population growth, and while difficult to separate the two, it is important to recognize the nature of this disaster that is unfolding and how it helps to explain the growing chaos across the world.

13

OUT OF BALANCE

Throughout scripture we find mention of the Lord's abhorrence to unjust, unfair, or manipulated and differing weights and measures. These verses all hold the same clear point. God hates imbalance.

False weights and unequal measures— the Lord detests double standards of every kind. **Proverbs 20:10 NLT**

False weights and unequal measures are a reference to a basic cheating method used in the marketplaces in ancient Israel all the way to Wall Street today. We have one price for selling and one price for buying when we place value on something. The value is based not upon fairness or accuracy but upon our own self-interest and ensures the other party we are doing business with is always at a disadvantage. It is a value and imbalance determined by deception. The person in power is changing the rules to gain more power, more wealth, and more security for himself – at the expense to those with less power. We all know that people will seek out their own interests and profit, but when the scales are out of balance something else has taken place. The system itself is rigged with an injustice that impacts everyone involved.

From the youth population bulge, to the food and water crises we will look at in the following sections of this book, this is a recurring theme found across the earth today. The system is out of order. It is out of balance. There is too much weighted toward the advantages of the haves and too little toward the have nots of the world. This observation is not an attack on capitalism and free markets. It is also not a suggestion that redistribution and collective ownership are the answers to the world's problems. They aren't. This is a recognition that our global system is plagued with imbalance. Sight of this imbalance is key to understanding the toppling chaos occurring all around us today.

The imbalance within the global systems of order today is not natural. It is brought on by deliberate human tactics flawed by deception and injustice. The youth population bulge and its consequences in places like Egypt, Nigeria, Pakistan, and others is not the result of mere cultural differences. It is the result of systemic mechanisms that stifled opportunity and access to the generation coming of age today. The United States once had a youth population bulge. It was called the Baby Boom and occurred as US servicemen returned from World War 2 and built families with their wives. One statistic suggests that at the height of the Baby Boom a child was born every 7 seconds. But this generation grew up with access to opportunities and promise. They were educated. They were fed and housed. They went to war and ended war. They inherited a national and economic infrastructure which allowed them to grow healthy and prosperous. The system worked for them.

Our leaders and statesmen explain that if Africa and Asia and other parts of the world facing unrest and chaos today would merely adopt the economic and political systems of the United States, from free markets to democracy, then their children also would reap the benefits of health and prosperity. This familiar narrative however is built upon a deception. It fosters a mentality that separates us (those who built their society right) from them (those who built their society wrong). It allows us to blame the victims of the growing chaos in the world today as contributors to their own demise. But it fails to account for the part played by the US and other great powers in the course of that last century to retard development and growth in the nations collapsing into chaos today.

When we review the history of the world from a wider perspective than our own personal context, we see that even while the Baby Boomers were coming of age, the US and Soviet Union were using other nations of the world as pawns in Cold War politics. Coups, assassinations and massive economic interference occurred throughout the world and obstructed the development of governments and economies that are imploding today. International institutions and private organizations from the World Bank to the International Monetary Fund to Goldman Sachs played outsized roles in disempowering national economies to the benefit of geopolitical superpowers like the United States, not to mention its investors. When we dig into nearly every economic and geopolitical crisis since World War 2 we find this behavior and activity. The messages of free markets and democracy were being preached from the podiums of the United Nations, but hidden hands were always tipping the scales in favor of those in power and against those in search of power. The game was rigged! The weights were imbalanced!

False weights and unequal measures— the Lord detests double standards of every kind. **Proverbs 20:10 NLT**

The systems upon which the nations and civilizations of the world rest share this inherent characteristic that is in opposition to the standards and designs of God. The Lord detests imbalance. There are two ways to understand what it means when the Lord *'detests'* something. The first interpretation suggests the pending judgment of God upon an imbalanced system. The fury of God will be unleashed against those who have not followed His way. Another perspective, and one which I see as more fitting to our current context of chaos, is the inevitable chaos that results when we build a system or way of life outside the standards and design of God. In this light, the chaos of collapse we are witnessing around the world today is not the result of God's fury and wrath but the consequences of building incorrectly. The global system is built upon faulty foundations, which makes its collapse inevitable.

If a man and woman marry but then commit ongoing acts of adultery, the marriage is doomed to fail. It fails not merely because God is angry with them. The marriage fails because there is a standard and specific architecture from God that defines how a marriage should be built. Central to that architecture and design are faithfulness and covenant. Likewise, when the order of the global system enters into a state of collapse, it is not necessarily because God is angry. The system was built upon an architecture of imbalance and injustice. The collapse is therefore inevitable. God detests imbalance and injustice because lives, families, societies and civilizations suffer under the burden of this corrupted system.

Throughout our world today, in almost every system upon which the globe is organized, there is imbalance and injustice. The system is wobbling. That is the chaos we are experiencing. And the end of the world is inevitable because that system cannot endure and it will collapse.

PART III

FAMINE AND FEAST – THE GLOBAL FOOD CRISIS

Global food and nutrition security is a major global concern as the world prepares to feed a growing population on a dwindling resource base, in an era of increased volatility and uncertainty.
World Economic Forum 2013[1]

Global demand for food is on the rise, driven by unprecedented growth in the world's population and widespread shifts in consumption patterns as countries develop. The Food and Agriculture Organization (FAO) projects that global agricultural production will need to more than double by 2050 to close the gap between food supply and demand. As this chronic pressure increases, the food system is becoming increasingly vulnerable to acute shocks.
Lloyd's Emerging Risk Report 2015[2]

*People do not despise a thief if he steals to satisfy his hunger when he is starving. Yet if he is caught, he must pay sevenfold, though it costs him all the wealth of his house. **Proverbs 6:30-31***

---

1. **World Economic Forum** . *Achieving the New Vision for Agriculture: New Models for Action.* A report by the World Economic Forum's New Vision for Agriculture initiative Prepared in collaboration with McKinsey & Company. Geneva : World Economic Forum , 2013.

2. **Maynard, Trevor.** *Food System Shock Emerging Risk Report – 2015.* Lloyd's. London : Lloyd's, 2015.

14

A DILEMMA AND A DIVIDE

I n early 2017, the Secretary General of the United Nations warned that 20 million people were at risk of famine, including 1.4 million children at imminent risk of death[1]. In Yemen alone at that time, 7 million people were on the brink of starvation while two-thirds of the population was relying upon humanitarian aid to survive. Every 10 minutes a Yemeni child was dying, and food deprivation was the leading cause[2]. The United Nations humanitarian chief Stephen O'Brien said at the time, "We are standing at a critical point in history. Already at the beginning of the year we are facing the largest humanitarian crisis since the creation of the United Nations."[3]

The World Food Programme reported in 2019 that 1 in 3 people around the world suffer from malnutrition. In the developing world, 12.9 percent of the population is undernourished. Poor nutrition is the leading cause of death for children around the world under the age of five, accounting for nearly 45 percent of deaths in this age bracket – that's 3.1 million children. One in four of the world's children is underweight. That number increases to one in three in the developing world.

In a nation like Yemen, torn apart by war, corruption, and chaos, families frequently must choose whether to use what little financial resources they have to buy medical supplies for their weakest children or to buy scraps of food for those that remain strong. A spokesman for the organization Action Against Hunger reported regarding these Yemeni children in 2016, "This is an entire generation at risk here."[4] Even when food can be found, it is frequently the wrong kind of food, providing the calories to keep bodies alive but providing no nutrients, thus ensuring malnourishment, future health issues, and physical deformities. By 2018, three years into the war in Yemen, the organization Save the Children reported that 85,000 children under the age of five had already starved to death there [5]. According to a Reuters report, mothers were being forced to leave their children to starve.

> "If a family does not have the necessary economic resources to feed the entire family then they will select who to feed. Sometimes you get up to a point where a mother is literally forced not to feed certain members of the family, most probably the youngest one."
> *Reuters*[6]

Travel to South Sudan, and you'll see guerillas and terrorist groups raid the food supplies of non-governmental organizations and relief agencies. The food arrives in the war-torn country only to be looted by the bad guys. As a result, many of the refugees living in displacement camps are forced to leave the shelter of the camps to search for food. This task generally falls upon the women and unveils yet another aspect of the horrible chaos in South Sudan. The militias are using hunger as a weapon against the people. When women leave the camps in search of food for their families, they are frequently captured by the militias, raped and beaten; then those who live are returned to the camp. Upon returning they live under the stigma of the rape while they and their children continue to starve[7]. In early 2019, Human Rights Watch detailed multiple accounts where women were gang raped at security check points near Beintu as they attempted to go to the markets to secure food rations for their families[8].

To the east, the small nation of Bangladesh in south Asia already had one of the highest starvation rates in the region before the Rohingya refugees began arriving in 2016 and 2017. In Myanmar the Rohingya people were facing ethnic cleansing from the nation's military. Their food supply was specifically targeted. Markets were shut down. Farms were burned. In their flight from the advancing government troops, many of the Rohingya were slaughtered in reported massacres. People who survived were separated from their families and many died in the mass exodus of almost 1 million Rohingya refugees across the border. There were no aid agencies. There were no supermarkets. Men, women, children, and the elderly survived on rainwater and grass or other plants found along their escape routes.

These are the stories, statistics, and scenarios for millions of people around the world suffering under the unique weight of man-made famines in the 21st century. The injustice and tragedy are heightened when contrasted against the bizarre paradoxical experience and issues afflicting those in other parts of the world.

The Lands of Excess

While famine rages in one part of the world, in other parts obesity is climbing to record rates. The Centers for Disease Control and Prevention issued reports in 2016 detailing how the US obesity epidemic was getting worse, not better, in spite of numerous awareness and prevention efforts. In 2016, 40 percent of American women were obese. Obesity is defined as weight that is higher than what is healthy relative to height. Among all American adults, 38 percent are obese as are 17 percent of teenagers. More than 5 percent of men and 10 percent of women are morbidly obese, meaning they run a much higher risk of diseases related to their obesity. This is not only an American epidemic. From 1975 to 2014, the number of men and women around the world classified as obese rose from 105 million to 641 million. Half of the human race is expected to be obese by 2025 if these trends continue[9]. And by almost all accounts, the trends will continue because nothing seems to be working in the effort to stop this literal growth in humanity.

US GDP per capita in 2017 was nearly $60,000. This is simply the total economic output of the US divided by the number of citizens living in the US in a single year. Each individual citizen's share of the country's GDP varies in reality, but the effects of our collective society are enjoyed by all through paved roads, military defense, operating utilities and sanitation systems, and the list goes on. Contrast this against the GDP of the nations where famine is far more likely: 70 percent of Africa has a GDP per capita of $6,000 or less. In 2017, four nations in Africa had a GDP per capita of less than $1,000 a year. In Asia, 12 countries had GDP per capita of less than a tenth of the GDP per capita in the US. This signals a massive divide between those in the feast part of the world and those living in the famine part of the world, of which food scarcity is only one pervading issue.

FOR THOSE LIVING in areas of the world, primarily much of the northern hemisphere, where access to food is easy and distribution plentiful, we literally have almost any food (or other consumer product for that matter) available to us at the click of a button. While reading this book you can utilize your smartphone to have groceries of all kinds sent to your doorstep. Our food issues have more to do with convenience and finding the time to cook. That is why food service companies have begun offering weekly meals in a box. No longer do we need to grocery shop or select what we are going to eat for the week. We simply sign up for the automatic draft and the weekly meals are sent to our front door, needing only to be mixed and heated. The ideas of hunger and malnourishment do not really register with us. We eat all we like only to struggle with New Year's resolutions to work off the excess weight and girth.

Food crisis for these areas of the world is learning to turn away from easy junk foods and toward healthier whole foods. If and when we fail at this, however, the options of vitamins, supplements, surgeries, and medical advances will frequently compensate for our own lack of discipline and right choices. This is the life of abundance. Concepts of famine and low food supply are usually only understood through the lens of ancient history or a late-night infomercial featuring starving African children and a charity organization that desperately needs help. It is far away, desperate, but also separate from our existence.

Starvation versus obesity, famine versus feast; these may seem like separate issues, but they are not. They are two sides of the same issue: the growing food crisis in the 21st century. It is an issue of terrible division and injustice that is perpetuated by a global food system most of us take for granted. On one side we have excess and convenience. On the other side we have desperate want and brutally harsh lack of access. It is in the division between the two extremes where we find our true modern crisis that is upending the global order and will lead to massive global upheaval in the coming years.

---

1. **Sengupta, Somini.** Why 20 Million People Are on Brink of Famine in a 'World of Plenty'. *New York TImes.* [Online] New York Times, February 22, 2017. [Cited: January 31, 2018.] https://www.nytimes.com/2017/02/22/world/africa/why-20-million-people-are-on-brink-of-famine-in-a-world-of-plenty.html?partner=rss&emc=rss.
2. **Bearak, Max.** A child in Yemen dies every 10 minutes as humanitarian aid funding falls short, U.N. says. *Washington Post.* [Online] April 25, 2017. [Cited: January 31, 2018.] https://www.washingtonpost.com/news/worldviews/wp/2017/04/25/a-child-in-yemen-dies-every-10-minutes-as-humanitarian-aid-falls-short-by-85-u-n-says/?utm_term=.b659e97c1b25.
3. **BBC.** UN: World facing greatest humanitarian crisis since 1945. *BBC.* [Online] March 11, 2017. [Cited: January 31, 2018.] http://www.bbc.com/news/world-africa-39238808.
4. **Raghavan, Sudarsan.** In Yemen's war, trapped families ask: Which child should we save? *Washington Post.* [Online] November 30, 2016. [Cited: January 31, 2018.] https://www.washingtonpost.com/world/middle_east/in-yemens-war-trapped-families-ask-which-child-should-we-save/2016/11/30/c2240cf4-7d60-4132-989f-2128b077efbb_story.html?utm_term=.5e9553e97243.
5. **Karasz, Palko.** 85,000 Children in Yemen May Have Died of Starvation. *New York Times.* [Online] November 21, 2018. [Cited: 9 2019, June.] https://www.nytimes.com/2018/11/21/world/middleeast/yemen-famine-children.html.
6. **Elks, Sonia.** Yemeni mothers forced to choose which child starves, says aid

group. *Reuters.* [Online] December 13, 2018. [Cited: June 9, 2019.] https://www.reuters.com/article/us-yemen-conflict-children/yemeni-mothers-forced-to-choose-which-child-starves-says-aid-group-idUSKBN1OC2OC.

7. **Foltyn, Simona.** 'I begged them to kill me instead': women in South Sudan raped under nose of UN. *The Guardian.* [Online] July 29, 2016. [Cited: January 31, 2018.] https://www.theguardian.com/global-development/2016/jul/29/women-south-sudan-raped-un-compound-juba-kill-me-instead.

8. **Pur, Nyagoah Tut.** South Sudan: Does Juba Even Care About Protecting Girls From Sexual Violence? *Human Rights Watch.* [Online] February 11, 2019. [Cited: June 9, 2019.] https://www.hrw.org/news/2019/02/11/south-sudan-does-juba-even-care-about-protecting-girls-sexual-violence#.

9. **Fox, Maggie.** America's Obesity Epidemic Hits a New High. *NBC News.* [Online] NBC, June 7, 2016. [Cited: January 31, 2018.] https://www.nbcnews.com/health/health-news/america-s-obesity-epidemic-hits-new-high-n587251.

15

HOW WE SAVED THE WORLD

Human civilization's relationship to food supply has always been a relatively tense one. A delicate balance between food supply and growing population demand marks much of our history. The oldest recorded human history captures the disruptive nature of famines in dictating the development and movement of human population centers. The stories of the Hebrew patriarchs Abraham, Jacob, and Joseph in the book of Genesis all include references to famines that ultimately changed the course of the Jewish people, their religion, and modern history. The great wars between ancient Rome and Carthage were frequently fought over the food supplies of southern Europe and North Africa.

Recognition of this careful dance between food supply and population growth was what triggered the study and alarming predictions in the late 18th century by Thomas Malthus, which we previously discussed. Malthus foresaw that as the world's population continued to grow, it would be impossible for the food supply to keep pace. He was wrong, but his warning was influential and echoed for generations all the way to Paul Ehrlich in the 1960s. Ehrlich warned that it was not only food but also the compounding strains that the growing global population would place upon food and water supplies that

would bring about the collapse of humanity. In 1967, William and
Paul Paddock wrote Famine 1975! in which they warned that the
growing demands upon the food supply in India alone would soon,
within a decade at the time of their writing, bring about massive
global catastrophe. The two respected authors even recommended
food aid to India be suspended as such aid would merely keep the
subcontinent's people alive long enough to have more children and
thus worsen the effects of the problem for the rest of the world[1].

In spite of these doomsday warnings over hundreds of years,
however, the population has continued to grow, and the food
supply has grown with it. A casual search on Google today will still
result in numerous articles, reports and headlines from reputable
sources suggesting that global population is soon to surpass the
supply of food our planet can produce. The historical data does not
support this, though. While global population doubled in the
second half of the twentieth century, the world's food supply
tripled. According to the Food and Agriculture Administration of
the United Nations, every region of the world except Sub Saharan
Africa had a positive growth in food production from the 1970s to
the 2000s. While the 1970s had much higher production yields than
the 1990s, throughout the world much of that lower growth was the
result of self-imposed restraints to prevent supply gluts and
damages in the commodities market. For decades after World War
II, the United States used its own surpluses to support other
regions of the world once Americans had eaten all their growing
bellies could hold.

Ehrlich and the many other intellectual descendants of Malthus
missed an essential variable in their calculations forecasting the end
of the food supply and human civilization. They did not calculate for
the effects of human ingenuity and technological shifts. The economist Julian Simon pointed to this specific vulnerability in the
Malthus and Ehrlich predictions in his 1981 book The Ultimate
Resource. He argued that the world was not soon to end, because
doomsdayers and naysayers had forgotten about mankind's and the
world's ultimate resource: "...skilled, spirited and hopeful people who

will exert their will and imaginations for their own benefit, and so, inevitably, for the benefit of us all."[2]

Simon was proven correct. India was expected to collapse upon itself at the time of Malthus's writings but by the end of the 20th century, famine was far less frequent, and the world's largest democracy was successfully feeding itself. These shifts in the narrative were made because human beings took hold of their own destiny and changed the story.

One example in this massive shift in food supply technology came at the beginning of the 20th century when chemist Fritz Haber developed the Haber-Bausch Process. This technological breakthrough alone allowed crops to secure nitrogen out of the air and convert it into the fertilizer. A 1999 Nature International Journal of Science report designated this as the most important technological breakthrough of the 20th century, stating that it was the detonator for the population explosion, and without Haber-Baush nearly half the world would be in a state of starvation [3]. But that was merely the beginning of a whole century of technological advances in food and agriculture that enabled the food supply to stay far in front of the booming population growth.

Just as important to the breakthroughs in agriculture technology were the breakthroughs in distribution and access. Today the global food system supports an infrastructure capable of shipping food around the world, depositing it onto the shelves of our local grocery store and tables of our homes with such ease that we barely consider the modern marvel. Storage and distribution systems maintain the freshness and timely sell of fruit, meat, and vegetables throughout the world. My home state of Arkansas exports $1 billion of rice annually to markets in Canada, Mexico, Central America, Haiti, and Saudi Arabia. In fact, rice grown in the US accounts for 12 percent of the global export market[4]. Brazil is the largest beef exporter in the world, moving more than 1,850,000 metric tons of fresh quality beef across the planet in 2016. Meanwhile China and India are the world's largest fruit exporters. This is a global food supply system that has leveraged the advances in agricultural technology, open markets, and developments in both storage and distribution technologies to conquer fears of global population growth outstripping global food supply.

Why Are People Still Starving?

The world averted collapse in the 20th century because of human ingenuity. But something is still amiss. How is it possible that I can literally use my smartphone to order any type of food I want for delivery to my door, but we cannot consistently get food to the 20 million people in danger of starvation that the UN warned the world about in 2017? There are political answers to this question, but they do not get to the real root of the problem. Open markets and democracies do not equate to an end to world hunger. (A quick reflection upon our former case study of Egypt demonstrates this point.)

In fact, as we dig deeper into this question of the great divide we find the problems of the global food crisis are actually built into the solutions that helped us avert catastrophe in the last century. Inherent to the architecture of the modern global food system is the fact that one part of the world benefits at the expense of other parts of the world. This reality is far more complex than it appears on the surface. It is not as simple as one country eats all the corn and that means another country has no corn. The dynamics of the modern global economy must be included in the equation to understand why small sections of the planet are overfed while larger sections are malnourished. Since World War II, the global economy has grown more interconnected and interdependent than ever imagined. Understanding how that growth occurred and the power and control that were built into the system helps us explain the current predicament. And as was the case in our examination of the population crisis in Part 2, recognizing where the modern food crisis is most extreme in the world is as important as understanding how the crisis developed in the first place.

---

1. **Paarlberg, Robert.** *Food Politics.* New York : Oxford University Press , 2013.

2. For an enjoyable read regarding Julian Simon's perspective, do an internet search on his famous wager with Paul Ehrlich.

3. **Smil, Vaclav.** *Detonator of the population explosion.* s.l. : Nature International Journal of Science, 1999.

4. **Madlom, Kim.** Right as Grain: Arkansas Leads Nation in Rice Production. *Farm Flavor.* [Online] January 28, 2013. [Cited: June 1, 2019.] https://www.farmflavor.com/arkansas/arkansas-ag-products/right-as-grain-arkansas-leads-nation-in-rice-production/.

16

HOW WE RUINED THE WORLD – HISTORY OF THE MODERN GLOBAL FOOD SYSTEM

The end of World War II resulted in the near total destruction of Europe's powerful nations and the global complex of colonialism they erected over the course of the prior century. It was only a few years into the postwar period when Great Britain withdrew from almost all of its prized colonial holdings throughout the world. France followed. The rise of new and independent states from Africa to Asia in the late 1940s transitioned these areas of the world out of subordination to colonial powers and into the new post-war nation-state age.

Colonialism, for all its oppressive evils, was the mechanism by which the world and its various systems were held together until this time. The global order of everything from economy to food was coordinated through the links of colonial power, priorities, and networks. India, for example, had been seen as the jewel in the crown of the British Empire within the colonial system because of the sheer scale of resources the subcontinent provided to the wider empire. India's spices, jewels, textiles and manpower were all key resources empowering Britain to rule and fuel its armies and administrations throughout the rest of the world. Immediately after Indian and Pakistani independence (the subcontinent was split between Muslim and Hindu nationalists), a massive and chaotic period briefly ensued upon the people there. This chaos meant hunger, death, and deprivation for many citizens of the new nations. The driving force for these tragedies was not a lack of resource but a lack of organization and coordination in the vacuum left by the withdrawal of the British. Similar scenes were taking shape throughout the world at this time as colonialism collapsed. While the old colonized world convulsed under its new freedoms, however, a different type of chaos and deprivation unfolded in the war shattered cities of Europe. A legitimate and full-fledged famine was setting in there.

As colonialism collapsed, global power shifted to the United States. The US was the greatest beneficiary of World War II. It suffered least among all the great powers in terms of soldiers, civilians, and economic production. Prior to World War II the US economy lagged far behind France, the United Kingdom, Italy, the Soviet Union, and Japan. Its military, smaller than Portugal's, ranked 18th in the world. The war transformed the United States into what President Franklin Roosevelt called "the arsenal of democracy." As Europe lay in smoldering ruins, the postwar era created a vacuum in global power to be filled by a new American superpower as the only force that could stand against and stop the spread of Soviet influence from the east. Thus was born the bipolar world order between the two remaining great superpowers of the world, the United States and the Soviet Union, that would dominate the second half of the 20th century.

Among the foundational pieces of American foreign policy and spread of global power and influence after the war was the Marshall Plan. Named after the former general and President Truman's Secretary of State, the Marshall Plan extended more than $13 billion in US aid to rebuild western Europe after the war. This was a staggering figure at the time but reaped enormous dividends for the new superpower. In an effort to contest any temptation toward the orbit of Soviet communism, the US granted aid to western European nations who were still trying to get back on their feet after the war. Along with the aid came US influence and integration to the wider

European economies, setting up the foundations for the modern global economy and trade system.

Today it is hard to realize how devastated Europe was by World War II. It was not simply Germany that lay in ruins as a result of allied bombings. It was a multi-sided war that took place on the continent, with Germany, the Allies, and the Soviets playing different sides. The result of this chaos upon the agriculture and food systems was immense. Even after the war was concluded in many areas of Europe, warlords representing former and future political powers roamed freely and violently, oppressing and subjecting the European people. The aid of the Marshall Plan went far to restore order, stability, and a foundation for future strength within Europe. The food system was central to this restoration effort. In 1949 President Truman announced in his inaugural address:

"More than half the people of the world are living in conditions approaching misery. Their food is inadequate. They are victims of disease. Their economic life is primitive and stagnant. Their poverty is a handicap and a threat both to them and to more prosperous areas. For the first time in history, humanity possesses the knowledge and the skill to relieve the suffering of these people." [1]

That relief came in the form of the Marshall Plan and other aid packages, focusing first upon Europe but then upon the wider world. American farmers and investors soon found that aid was a lucrative business both directly and in the long-term lingering influence it brought to the American economy. To this day, many who complain of American foreign aid underestimate the indirect benefits the US economy receives from such initiatives. US aid meant US trade for farmers who were turning surpluses throughout America's agricultural sector. This boom in food exports from aid packages was so successful that by the mid 1950s European farmers and officials were actually pushing for the aid to stop. Europe was on the mend, and its farms were rebuilt by this time; but the continent's farmers could not turn a profit because US food aid was holding the prices artificially low. Raj Patel in his book Stuffed and Starved explains how this shift changed the shape of the global food system. As Europe demanded that food aid be halted, beginning in July 1954, "US food aid was pointed at a new target, one where farmers were politically much less able to make the same demands of the United States – the Global South."[2]

Benevolent Aid Becomes Pragmatic Economics

Two years later, food aid accounted for half of all US economic aid throughout the world. From the 1950s onward, food became a central piece of American aid throughout the world and a foundational element in the evolving US-dominated global economy. By 1960, one-third of the world's trade in wheat came from US food aid[3]. The intent of American aid in programs like the Marshall Plan was both politically pragmatic and morally benevolent. It took only a decade for the economic benefits of aid and the resulting trade networks it established to be recognized, and by that point US food aid was much more tightly linked to agricultural and economic lobbyist objectives.

A conundrum developed: US farmers were harvesting a crop surplus every year but struggled to turn these surpluses into profits due to limited market demand. The mouths of America were being filled, but there was still food left over – so food aid was again the answer. Food aid opened up new foreign markets, and those markets could be largely commanded by American policies.

In 1960, 70% of US wheat exports were distributed abroad as food aid rather than commercial sales [4]. As US wheat went into foreign markets, it was not sold and distributed in a free market economy. Prices were kept artificially low through government subsidies in order to make the wheat better available to the poor who were being aided. The unintended consequence of this practice, however, was a destabilizing effect upon local economies and agriculture systems south of the equator, where most of the food aid was going. Local farmers could not compete with US food supplies entering their country at artificially low prices, so they were soon driven out of business. The economies of these nations were thereby permanently underdeveloped and a constant demand for aid from the western world was built into them. We would soon learn that such economies and states were also highly susceptible to corruption and despotism.

Meanwhile, the US economy built a dependency upon these exports and sales to the poorer nations of the world. US farmers were actually being paid to grow fewer crops in the United States. The US needed to limit the surpluses from further increase because the government was already subsidizing so many food exports. The subsidizing of the food exports was holding crop prices low. If we kept adding to that surplus, prices would go even lower. The effects of this manipulation were felt strongest in the poorer nations receiving the food aid. They were being fed, but their economies were being destabilized and their internal systems that might have brought economic and agricultural restoration were being broken.

Raj Patel has compared the relationship between the US and the poorer nations of the world it was feeding at the time to that of a dealer and a junky, both caught in a cycle of mutual destruction from which they could not walk away and through which they would ultimately come to resent each other. The former benevolence of the food aid system had also faded by the time of the Nixon administration, and the pragmatic political strength of controlling the world's food system had taken a firm hold. In the words of Earl Butz, US Agriculture Secretary under Presidents Nixon and Ford, "Hungry men listen only to those who have a piece of bread. Food is a tool. It is a weapon in the US negotiating kit."

Modernizing the Global Economy Around Dysfunction

Much was to change in the 1970s, however, with a world energy crisis sparked by the OPEC embargo and sustained by the newly recognized global strength of the world's oil producing nations. Higher energy prices meant a recalibration of the world food system's supply flow. The US shifted its decades-old trend of feeding the poorer nations and began sending its food surpluses to the Soviet Union in exchange for the newly high-priced oil. Meanwhile, European nations advanced into the global south to fill the void left by the US. The poor nations of the southern hemisphere continued their addiction to artificially low-priced food imports even though they were neutralizing their domestic agriculture and economic systems, while the Europeans gained income off this new export market.

Then came the economic shocks of the energy crisis. Higher interest rates led to inflation throughout the world, and as the oil producing nations grew rich, the rest of the world was caught in an economic slump. The effects were felt strongest among nations whose economies had been retarded by the food aid system since the early 1960s. While the developed world of America and Europe waited in line for gas, much of the rest of the world needed money to buy food. The bulging bank accounts of the oil producing nations were all very happy to lend money – at high interest rates. By the end of the 1970s, this led to the worldwide economic recession that would devastate and collapse numerous economies throughout the southern hemisphere. This was the time period when we became more familiar with the plight of African children starving to death on nightly television infomercials as well as tales of collapsing economies and currencies in Latin America. They were both stories and byproducts of the same issue, although most observers did not recognize it at the time. The interconnected complexities of the global economy and the food system were being lost in most people's perspectives.

Borrowers Become Servants to the Lenders

Two significant factors contributed solutions to this crisis as well the perpetuation of the dysfunctional global food system. The first was strictly economic in its nature. Organizations like the World Bank offered bailouts and loans to the poor and weakened nations suffering most from the crises of the 1970s, explaining that the cause for all this suffering was due to poor economic structures and was their own doing. Loans and bailouts would be given, but only on the condition that economic reform take shape in these nations. (Recall how we saw this in our earlier case study on Egypt during the Bread Riots of the late 1970s under Anwar Sadat.) No consequences were dealt to the richer nations of the north who had assisted in retarding these economies with food aid, intentionally or not.

The bulk of these reforms were centered on free market principles and, in theory, would have worked well had the nations of the more developed world in the northern hemisphere been constrained to the same standards – but they were not. Tariffs and protectionist policies, as an example, were standard in nations like the United States while forbidden in those receiving loans from the World Bank. As a result, these debtor nations surrendered even more of their economic sovereignty, and a form of economical colonialism ensued.

THROUGHOUT THE NEXT FEW DECADES, a new system developed in which the agricultural systems among the debtor nations were revamped in order to pay back their loans from the 1980s. The nations who were now producing much of the world's food were not benefitting from it. The food grown in the global South was going to benefit the global North, but it was not uncommon for a nation operating as a leading crop producer to have many of its own citizens starving to death.

Brazil and Argentina are among the top soybean producing nations in the world today (behind the US). In Brazil, 35 percent of the population lives on less than $2 a day. In rural areas (farming areas), this increases to 51 percent[5]. According to Andrew MacMillan, former Director of the Food and Agriculture Organization (FAO), "Hunger is the most extreme manifestation of the huge problem of poverty in Brazil. Few people die of starvation, but there is widespread chronic food insecurity and malnutrition. This means that people are unable to produce or gain access to enough food of an adequate quality for a healthy life. It is the hunger of the missed meal, and it is very debilitating."[6] A 2011 BBC story noted a reporter traveling across miles of soybean fields to reach a village in Argentina where children were literally dying of malnutrition for lack of food [7]. This was happening in one of the world's largest food exporters.

In many countries where food exports are a dominant piece of the economy -- Thailand, Vietnam, and Kenya for example -- another symptom of this imbalance has set in. Children are not suffering from starvation but rather from obesity as processed junk foods are imported and exchanged for the domestic crops that export out to the rest of the world. Higher rates of diabetes, heart disease, and other health issues now afflict the youth of these nations where food and other agriculture products grow in abundance.

The Green Revolution

After the unique economic factors, the second solution to the crisis of these debtor nations in the early 1980s is known to history as the Green Revolution. The Green Revolution actually began earlier in the 1960s, but its transfer to the under-developed world was often hand in hand with economic reforms. It consisted of technological innovations that had worked to bring prosperity in the developed world of the North now being given to the nations of the South. The Green Revolution has been a mixed bag in its results. Professor Robert Paarlberg, a proponent of the Green Revolution, explained in his 2013 book Food Politics how the Green Revolution worked well in nations where the government adapted easily to free market reforms, but less well in nations where governments interfered in the market and agricultural system.

Critics of the Green Revolution see a different result. The technological innovations caused poor farmers to compete for land and water supplies to furnish massive farming initiatives which the Green Revolution policies encouraged. Also, farmers were no longer farming on the basis of what was most productive to their indigenous environments but according to what resulted in the greatest profits. This practice was often in direct contradiction to the capacities of their local climates and soils. As a result, this brought about a draining of local aquifers, erosion of the soil and a worsening of the environmental conditions needed to grow food. In other words, the short-term gains of the Green Revolution for many parts of the world was a profit, but the long-term loss was a landscape no longer capable of bringing forth food. This was occurring in nations and societies where agriculture had been the foundation of the culture and economy for millennia.

Further, to access the technologies of the Green Revolution, the farmers of the poor nations had to indebt themselves to the businesses and technologies of the richer nations in the northern part of the world. While many farmers held out against this trend, insisting on their own methods of farming to be more sustainable long-term, they soon discovered they could not compete with the scale and depth of production that the indebted farmers of the Green Revolution were experiencing. Meanwhile, those who took the bait, signed the loans, and entered into loan contracts found they had entered into a modern-day indentured servanthood contract with which their lands and work could not keep pace. In many instances, farmers have lost their farms to industrial farm conglomerates when they could not repay their debts. In order to feed their family, these farmers go to work for the businesses that have conquered them as hired contract labor on the same lands once owned and worked by their fathers and their father's father.

The results of this system have produced a global South that serves as a plantation to the global North's supercenters and dinner tables. The individual farmer has been supplanted by the industrialized farm. The soil and climate are benefitting the more prosperous homes and nations of the world until they are dried up and there is nothing left. Thus, we find the incredibly complex global food system to be infested with inequities that appear impossible to extract. It is in these nations and societies, where inequities are most pronounced and resentment is most felt, that corruption and authoritarianism thrive. Civil unrest follows and the manmade famines of the 21st century are commonplace.

The world food system is thus caught in a global dilemma. On the one hand we have corruption, upheaval, and oppression that lead to famine of mass proportions, but on the other hand we have a managed and modern industrialized food system that leads consumers into excess and obesity – even as it simultaneously drives the poorest of the world into systemic poverty and more hunger. The extremes feed one another, accelerating the divide between them. We have starvation and obesity operating side by side and little can be done about it. The real issue is not what Malthus or Ehrlich feared it would be. The world population has not outstripped its food supply. The issue is the way food is accessed in this global system that is strangling parts of the world. The devices of man's own making have separated a large portion of the globe into the haves and have-nots. The interconnectedness of the system that resolved the food crisis after World War II held within it the very mechanisms to perpetuate injustice, resentment, and insecurity around the world. As these byproduct of the global food system spread they bring with them unrest and upheaval around the world.

1. **Truman, Harry.** Truman's Inaugural Address. *Harry S. Truman Presidential Library and Museum.* [Online] January 20, 1949. https://www.trumanlibrary.org/whistlestop/50yr_archive/inagural20jan1949.htm.
2. **Patel, Raj.** *Stuffed and Starved.* Brooklyn : Melville House, 2012.
3. **Patel, Raj.** *Stuffed and Starved.* Brooklyn : Melville House, 2012.
4. **Paarlberg, Robert.** *Food Politics.* New York : Oxford University Press, 2013.
5. **IFPRI.** Brazil. *Food Security Portal* . [Online] 2012. [Cited: January 31, 2018.] http://www.foodsecurityportal.org/brazil.
6. **Food and Agriculture Organization of the United Nations Newsroom.** Brazil: The hunger of the missed meal. *Food and Agriculture Organization of the United Nations Newsroom.* [Online] February 14, 2003. [Cited: January 31, 2018.] http://www.fao.org/english/newsroom/news/2003/13320-en.html.
7. **BBC.** Dying from hunger in food-exporting Argentina. *BBC.* [Online] April 6, 2011. [Cited: January 31, 2018.] http://www.bbc.com/news/world-latin-america-12973543.

17

2008 GLOBAL FOOD CRISIS – A CASE STUDY

T he 2008 Global Food Crisis serves as an icon to the complexity, fragility, and dangers inherent with the global food system. In a year when much of the western world was captivated by the global economic meltdown and the election of Barak Obama as President of the United States, the rest of the world was being forced to confront a very different kind of crisis and historical transition. Throughout much of the developing world, men and women were encountering a terribly real and dangerous global food crisis. The price of basic food staples more than doubled, triggering unrest around the planet. In Egypt and Pakistan there were food riots. Violent protests sprang up in Cameroon, Mauritania, Ivory Coast, Ethiopia, Yemen, Uzbekistan, Thailand, Indonesia, Philippines and Italy. After more than a week of violent protests in response to the rise of food prices, the president of Haiti was removed from office.

This was one of the most widespread global crises in the early years of the 21st century. It happened relatively suddenly, and had it not been eclipsed by the economic meltdown in the United States and Europe we would surely be talking more about it today. Between 2005 and 2011, the price of wheat rose 115 percent, rice 102 percent, and maize (corn) 204 percent. In a nation such as Pakistan, where the average family spends 41 percent of their income on food[1], these price spikes were devastating.

Initial reports and analyses suggested the global food crisis was triggered by rising populations and food demand in the developing world. The Chinese were becoming more prosperous, so they were eating more like their American counterparts. In an interconnected globalized economy, the flutter of a butterfly's wings in one part of the world can set off a tidal wave of chaos in another part of the world. In addition, the rise of India's middle class was thought to have triggered higher rates of food consumption that caused a shock to the global food system as well. At best, these speculations were only partially correct. In the immediate aftermath of the 2008 Global Food Crisis, papers and policy proposals were drafted by all of the world's leading food organizations. These sought to explain what had occurred, yet frequently disagreed in their diagnoses, giving light to how complex and confusing the world's system of food supply and distribution had become.

Identifying the origins of the crisis demonstrates how unprepared the world was for subsequent shocks. In 2010 the Washington DC think tank International Food Policy Research Institute issued a study and report[2] on the food crisis to identify its primary causes. Among the key causes: a growing demand for agrofuels which drove up the price of corn and soybeans; then higher oil prices at the time further increased the demand for such biofuels. It was a vicious cycle that was destroying the global food markets. Why grow food for physical human consumption when so much more money could be made from growing food for fuels.

The US Energy Acts of 2005 and 2007 mandated the consumption of agrofuels. This was a popular move domestically, signaling the US's move to energy independence objectives. Rather than relying on oil from foreign lands, the US would create alternative fuels domestically. What better place to start than those massive corn fields of the Midwest that had produced so much surplus for decades that farmers were paid to grow fewer, not more, crops? Agrofuel consumption goals in the US grew from 4 billion to 7.5 billion annually, and then surged to 36 billion gallons a year. Thus was born an agrofuel boom! Between 2001 and 2007 the amount of corn used in US ethanol distilleries increased from 17 million tons to 81 million tons. As more corn was planted to feed this agrofuel demand, wheat and soybean crops were displaced, lowering their supply and increasing their demand and also their price[3].

The agrofuel boom drove up the costs of agriculture, triggering panic buying around the world. According to a report issued by the Institute for Food and Development Policy, "in 2007 the jump in ethanol production more than doubled the average annual growth in demand for the world's grains that took place between 1990 and 2005."

Meanwhile, weather issues in Australia, Argentina, and Ukraine further added to the tightening global food supply. As fewer crops were available for the dining room table in the northern hemisphere, those nations began replacing them from the southern hemisphere. Imagine a great vacuum sucking the world's supply of grains from the southern hemisphere and into specific geographies and economies within the northern hemisphere. This was what the US move to agrofuels triggered in 2007, resulting in lower food supply and higher food prices for those in the southern part of the globe who were reaping none of the highlighted benefits of American energy independence.

It should be stressed that this was not conspiratorial but simply the effects of unintended consequences by the world's largest economy within an incredibly complex global food system. As riots and unrest were brewing in Pakistan and Egypt, the rising prices were benefitting the large producers of the north. At the time of the food crisis, Archer Daniels Midland, Cargill, and Bunge controlled the world's grain supply, while Monsanto controlled three-fifths of the global seed production. The 2008 Food Crisis brought a 20 percent jump in profits in the final quarter of 2007 for Archer Daniels Midland, 45 percent for Monsanto, and 60 percent for Cargill (57).

All these issues together were the real driving forces behind the 2008 global food crisis. When Egyptians protested in the streets, when Haitians were making biscuits out of yellow clay, vegetable oil and salt, it was in large part the indirect consequence of farmers in Nebraska selling their corn crops for agrofuels. It was also the result of bad weather among the world's largest global grain producers. And it was the result of the global food system being so interwoven with the global economy.

Ironically, what stopped this crisis from worsening was the 2008 economic meltdown triggered by collapsing debt bubbles in the US and Europe. When the world's largest economies were teetering on the edge of collapse, their governments kicked in with government bailouts and historically low interest rates. The low interest rates changed the nature of the food crisis, loosening the belts of global food supply and opening easier access to the demand for food among poorer nations. This resulted in a rapid lowering of food prices and an end to the crisis. Once again, unintended consequences were as much a part of the solution to the global food crisis in 2007 and 2008 as they were a part of the creation.

This is the reality of the global food system and its vulnerable supply which the world relies upon. It is highly susceptible to both manmade and environmental issues. This complexity and the changing nature of human civilization places a global food catastrophe near the top of the list of issues which will likely and almost certainly impact the globe in the next fifty years. Today, the world's leading insurers are preparing commodity houses and brokers for future shocks to the food system. Almost every significant monitor of the global food system has warned that 2008 is a sign of things to come rather than an anomaly.

Many commentators have suggested that events such as the Arab Spring that swept through the Middle East and North Africa after 2012 were an effect of the 2008 food crisis. To that end, leaders and governments in much of the underdeveloped world have recalibrated their postures and policies to secure themselves and their power in the event of future food shocks and crises. The state of affairs today in North Africa and Syria can be traced back to this global event and demonstrate the dangers that lie ahead for the world: the vulnerability of the global food system and the political repercussions that roll out from any shock to the system.

---

1. **Plumer, Brad.** Map: Here's how much each country spends on food. *Vox.* [Online] August 19, 2015. [Cited: January 11, 2018.] https://www.vox.com/2014/7/6/5874499/map-heres-how-much-every-country-spends-on-food.

2. **Fan, Derek Headey and Shenggen.** *Reflections on the Global Food Crisis How Did It Happen? How Has It Hurt? And How Can We Prevent the Next One?* International Food Policy Research Institute. Washington DC : International Food Policy Research Institute, 2010.

3. **Peabody, Eric Holt-Giménez and Loren.** *From Food Rebellions to Food Sovereignty: Urgent call to fix a broken food system.* Oakland : Institute for Food and Development Policy - Food First, 2008.

18

MODERN FAMINE

For a great duration of human history, famine was the terrible dread that kings and priests could neither contend with nor prevent. It is thought to have upended and destroyed many ancient civilizations we know little about today. Around the time of the industrial revolution, however, the narrative and man's relation to famine and food crisis began to shift. More modern planning techniques and agriculture technology made the food supply, if not controllable, at least more manageable.

Recently the World Peace Foundation at the Fletcher School at Tufts University presented a study into the causes and nature of food crises brought on by famine since 1870[1]. Their findings were enlightening and show not only the changing relationship between human civilization and the food supply but the inherent risks that remain. Between 1870 and 2015, famine and forced mass starvation have killed more than 116 million people around the world. Until 1970 that figured included an average of more than 1 million people per year. Since 1980 there has been a significant decline in the number of deaths resulting from famine. Notice that this has occurred even while the global population has increased dramatically since that time.

Famine in the Imperial System

The Tufts report described three distinct periods of famines and food crises that occurred since 1870. The first period, lasting from 1870 to the early 20th century, consisted of the late imperialist era where native populations were forced into the global colonial system, always in a subordinate position. For example, the Indian subcontinent endured several famines during this time period even while the farmers there helped fill pantries of the wider British Empire. Between the 1870s and 1901, the people of India endured no less than four widespread famines killing more than 12 million people. In each of these Indian famines, the leading causes were drought and colonial management practices -- sometimes deliberate and sometimes out of ignorance.

China was host to the most severe and frequent famines during this period. An 1876-79 famine claimed no fewer than 9 million lives. Once again in 1897-1901, another Chinese famine killed an additional 1 million people through starvation. Internal rebellions, oppressive colonial practices, and a disruption of the local economies and food supply for the wider British Empire were key instigators in these events.

Africa rounds out the top three regions of the world with the most severe famines during the period of colonial imperialism. Ethiopia experienced the deaths of more than 1 million people in a famine lasting from 1889-92. Congo lost more than 5 million people in a brutal famine lasting from 1885-99. In the events of both nations, the underlying cause was oppression and mismanagement by way of colonialism, along with the resulting wars and domestic unrest.

War and Totalitarianism Famine

The second era of modern famine spanned the time frame of the two world wars and is marked by war and totalitarianism. This period marked the greatest era of mass starvation in the history of the world. Whole races of people were literally subjected to annihilation by way of starvation - genocide. Dictators like Stalin and Hitler used food as a weapon of war for killing millions.

The communist revolution in Russia led to a massive famine where more than 9 million people starved to death in 1922. In Ukraine between 1932-33, Joseph Stalin unleashed what has come to be known as Terror Famine. He instituted policies and actions to deliberately starve the people of Ukraine to death. Food supplies were confiscated, supply routes severed, and crops destroyed. All of this was a means for Stalin to put down political independence movements in the country. Through the course of the 1930s and World War II, much of Eastern Europe was caught in a similar crossfire between Hitler and Stalin. Starvation was used literally as a weapon of war between the powers of Germany and the Soviet Union. Poland saw the death of more than 3 million people. Germany and the USSR saw the death of 4.2 million people on their borderlands through these hunger wars.

Even as this terror was unfolding in Europe, Asia was not immune to the continuing crisis of famine brought about by war, oppression, and civil unrest. Between 1934-37 more than 5 million died by famine in China's Sichuan province. The Japanese invasion of China triggered the starvation and death of another 1.5 million people. Meanwhile 2.4 million starved to death in Indonesia while living, or rather dying, under Japanese occupation. India was never taken by the Japanese and remained under British control throughout World War II, but mismanagement and wartime policy here fostered yet another massive famine on the subcontinent where 2.1 million people starved to death in Bengal.

Nationalist Famine

The final era includes the communist period of rule, where great famines unfolded in China and Cambodia. The great famines produced by policies and strategies of the likes of Mao Tse Tung resulted in the deaths of tens of millions of his own citizens. Between 1958-62 Mao instituted his program known as The Great Leap

Forward. It was intended to transform China in a short 5-year time span into a competitor to the great and powerful nations of the world. Chinese culture was upended. At least 45 million people perished as a result. As many as 32 million of these victims died of starvation. While Chinese citizens starved to death, Mao used the country's grain supplies to pay back loans to the Soviet Union as well as to offer assistance to poverty-stricken third world nations. The Chinese countryside and agriculture system was emptied and its people left to starve. The Great Leap Forward was an abysmal failure, but the communist attention to detail and bureaucracy was at least careful to document the infamously brutal debacle.

In the 1970s, the Khmer Rouge led by the dictator Pol Pot overthrew the ruling power and instituted their Year Zero policy. All history prior to the revolution was made irrelevant and the country was to start from zero and rebuild under Pol Pot. While the nation's elite were executed, millions from the cities were forced to the countryside to build an agriculturally based utopia. Around 1.7 million Cambodian people died under Pol Pot's murderous rule, many by way of starvation through famine brought by the dictator's absurd policies.

Modern Famine

Throughout the 20th century, when the average person thought of modern famine, they thought of eastern Europeans and Asians. The issues were largely brought under manageable control by the 1980s, however, and the drop off in famine there continued to 2016 thanks to a better coordinated global food supply as well as greater democratic and stabilized governments throughout these formerly starving parts of the world. There was also a rise in humanitarian and non-governmental organizations (NGOs) which, when conditions for famine did arise, could be quickly dispatched for aid and relief, empowered and funded by organizations like the United Nations.

It was not until the 1980s that nations in Africa became associated with famine in the popular media and cultural mindset. Today, when most Westerners think of Africa they think of starving babies and their mothers as featured on various commercials for non-profits seeking to feed the hungry in Africa. These advertisements became a staple of cable television and largely shaped the image of Africa throughout the western world today.

Man Made Famines

A few key insights stand out from this 150-year overview of the great famines around the world. Most significant among these is that the leading cause for the major famines around the world since 1870 was and still is the hand of man itself. Droughts and natural disasters have contributed to major famines over the course of modern history, but none were the result of drought alone. They always included the interfering hand of government policies, violent warlords and dictators, or arrogant and oppressive imperialists. This subtle underlying fact holds true today. In all of the places where famine is taking hold, the hand of man can be directly identified as a major component in the cause and duration of the famine.

At the beginning of Part 3 of this book, I noted the 2017 UN alert that 20 million were at risk of famine. The nations at most severe risk at that time included Yemen, Somalia, South Sudan, and Nigeria. In each of these countries war, civil war, and insurgencies were at work, both worsening the crisis and causing it to last longer. Other nations not included in the alert but still at great risk to famine and starvation that same year were Congo, Central African Republic, Libya, Iraq, Syria and Afghanistan. All had the same on-the-ground reality. Modern famine is not caused by blight and drought -- it is caused by war, violence, and warlords. In places like Nigeria and South Sudan, the effects of famine can literally be isolated to the specific internal geographic regions where insurgencies and terrorism are operating at the highest levels.

It is not only violence and warfare though. It is also the interfering hand of incompetent rulers and powerbrokers. Venezuela was once among the most thriving economies in South America thanks to its vast oil reserves. Today it is suffering from crisis in which a diminishing food supply is only one component. Thanks to the irresponsible economic policies of Hugo Chavez and his successor Nicolas Maduro, inflation has destroyed the economy. In a January 2018 Washington Post article, Francisco Toro wrote: "In fact, as Venezuela sinks deeper and deeper into the first hyperinflation the Western Hemisphere has seen in a generation, bolivar banknotes have come to be worth basically nothing: Each bill is worth about $0.0001 at the current exchange rate, meaning you need to have 100 of them to equal one penny."[2] Looting has replaced commerce. Barter and trade have replaced currency. Stores cannot afford to stock their shelves; but neither can consumers afford to purchase from those shelves. More than 10 million parents in October of 2017 were skipping at least one meal a day. Seventy five percent of Venezuelans lost an average of 19 pounds in the year of 2017 alone. One in 12 Venezuelans scavenged for food in the trash bins outside of restaurants. Ten percent of the children living in this crashing economy are suffering from malnutrition. The school system is collapsing because students do not have the energy normally furnished by caloric intake to make it through a whole school day. Even if they could, teachers are leaving school early to stand in line for food rations[3].

Another example of the incompetency of rulers is Zimbabwe. Zimbabwe was once considered the breadbasket of Africa. In 1980 Robert Mugabe was elected to the Presidency – a seat he would hold until 2017. Mugabe initiated a series of land and agricultural reforms that wound up wrecking the economy and the food supply. Maize farming which stood at 1.5 million tons before 2000 dropped to 500,000 tons by 2003. Wheat dropped from 309,000 tons to 27,000 tons [4]. The farming system collapsed. The ranks of the poor grew. The people starved.

Modern day famines still occur, but unlike those of ancient history they are not the result of drought, climate change, or crop failures. Such issues can all play a role, but the hand of man itself plays the leading role in modern famine. Through violence, oppression, domestic instability, or simply incompetence, more famine and widespread starvation has occurred due to the heavy and interfering hand of man than nature in the last 150 years. There is no reason to believe this trend will change. This realization was partly what led Alex De Waal, executive director of the World Peace Foundation and a leading expert on international famine, to recently ask if the great era of famines was really over. [5]

The word "famine" brings about dread and provocation for public response, but the bulk of the world's hungry people are not living in famine conditions. They are underfed, undernourished, and almost unheard victims to a problem much more complex, far more widespread, and virtually invisible to those living in the overfed parts of the world. They also happen to occupy the parts of the planet where the population crisis in part two of this book is most severe. If we overlay a map of the areas of the world where the youth population bulge is most acute with a map of where hunger and conditions leading to famine are most severe, we will find them nearly identical. Where they are not identical, it can be argued that their discrepancies represent areas where one crisis is spreading into another crisis in a neighboring country. An overpopulated area of Nigeria might translate to refugees fleeing across the border into a neighboring country that is less stable -- and this triggers the political conditions that lead to a food crisis.

Man Made Inequity

The current level of food crisis we are experiencing is different from that of the prior 150 years for several reasons. First, we have the supply and distribution networks to prevent this crisis – but it is not being prevented. Second, the hand of man is uniquely apparent in both the making of famines at one end of the food crisis spectrum and obesity epidemics at the other end of the spectrum. Our current food crises demonstrate the inequities of the modern global order more effectively than anything we have witnessed in human history. Former food crises under colonial or war conditions could be isolated to specific areas of the globe. Today's conditions are spreading throughout the world, isolated only by the polarized divide between the haves and the have nots. The threats and crisis are compounded by the underlying issues of population threats. As we have already seen in so many locations where hunger and famine are most severe, insurgent and terrorist groups upset and destroy systems of aid and relief meant to assist those dying of starvation.

This is what it looks like when the world is falling apart and coming to an end. Because the core issue in the modern food crises is not climate change or a lack of supply but the hand of man, we can reasonably anticipate the crises to intensify and spread. As the gap between the haves and the have nots of the world, between those living in conditions of feast and those in conditions of famine, continue to intensify and spread, the repercussions of the food crises will grow. Arab Spring, the Syrian Civil War, the collapse of the Middle East and North Africa, the Rohingya genocide, and the list goes on...all of these great tragedies and human catastrophes of only the second decade of the 21st century are disasters driven forward by exploding human population and food crisis. This is only the beginning!

---

1. **World Peace Foundation** . Famine Trends Dataset, Tables and Graphs. *The Fletcher School Tufts University World Peace Foundation.* [Online] World Peace Foundation, January 11, 2018. [Cited: January 11, 2018.] https://sites.tufts.edu/wpf/famine/.

2. **Toro, Francisco.** In Venezuela, money has stopped working. *Washington Post.* [Online] January 18, 2018. [Cited: January 31, 2018.] https://www.washingtonpost.com/news/democracy-post/wp/2018/01/17/in-venezuela-money-has-stopped-working/?utm_term=.d4a3a40179fa.

3. **Panzarella, Tim.** As Food Crisis Continues, Venezuelans Turn to American Friends and Relatives for Help. *Reason.* [Online] October 24, 2017. [Cited: January 31, 2018.] http://reason.com/blog/2017/10/24/as-venezuelans-scrounge-for-food-sociali.

4. **Power, Samantha.** How To Kill A Country. *Atlantic Magazine.* [Online] December 2003. [Cited: January 31, 2018.] https://www.theatlantic.com/magazine/archive/2003/12/how-to-kill-a-country/302845/.

5. **Waal, Alex De.** Is the Era of Great Famines Over? . *New York Times.* [Online] May 8, 2016. [Cited: January 31, 2018.] https://www.nytimes.com/2016/05/09/opinion/is-the-era-of-great-famines-over.html.

PART IV

PARCHED AND DROWNING – THE GLOBAL WATER CRISIS

"Water is your body's principal chemical component and makes up about 60 percent of your body weight. Your body depends on water to survive. Every cell, tissue and organ in your body needs water to work properly."
Mayo Clinic

Water scarcity already affects every continent. Water use has been growing globally at more than twice the rate of population increase in the last century, and an increasing number of regions are reaching the limit at which water services can be sustainably delivered, especially in arid regions.
United Nations

19

EXTREME DIVIDES

So far, we have looked at the global population and food crises that are compounding in scale and severity across the globe. In and of themselves, these are terrible disasters posing enormous threats to the world, but alone they are not enough to support the end of the world reality that is the basis of this book. More significant than the individual crisis is the fundamental driver growing and perpetuating it. The driving forces of each crisis are division and polarization, which in turn increases the scale and scope of each disaster.

For example, the population crisis is worsening not merely because of rising birth rates but because of the widening income gap. The population crisis is feeding civil wars, riots, refugee camps, terrorism, and more. At the root of these geopolitical emergencies is a population bulge frustrated by the easily seen and ever widening gap between the haves and have-nots.

Similarly, the food crisis is not only about famine or supply needs. These have always existed, and in fact we found the technology to conquer them in the last century. The greater crisis is the levels of injustice and inequity built into the global food system, strangling many parts of the world with starvation and economic impairment while other parts of the world drown in excess. It is the levels of extreme imbalance at work in the world that are driving these crises to worsening effects every year. They are no longer contained to specific borders, nations, and regions of the world. The crisis is spreading through the consequences of these imbalances. Whole regions of Africa and Asia are collapsing under the weight of these crises. That trend will continue and soon impact Europe and the Americas, if not directly then indirectly through migration of those affected.

None of the crises we observe in these pages better captures the image of division and inequity that is driving global disasters than that of the global water crisis. In one part of the world, cities and states are literally sinking under an excess of water. In other parts of the world, the wells are literally running dry. One people are saturated while another people are parched. One coastline is sinking under rising ocean waters while another land is collapsing into sinkholes as subterranean aquifers dry out.

Our familiarity with either side of this crisis is usually based upon where we live. Those in the Northern Hemisphere are more aware of the rising waters crisis, while those in the Southern Hemisphere fear the lack of water. This story should be told as one, however, for us to truly appreciate the magnitude of what is being experienced on our planet today. The conditions of the earth are literally screaming the dangers of division and inequity that are so familiar to our existence today. We miss the message so frequently because it is interpreted through divisive political language. The facts are plain to see, however. The world is being torn apart in the imbalance of the great divides of space, food, and finally that basic element of human life – water.

20

SINKING IN EXCESS

T hroughout the world in major cities and dense population centers, the world's oceans are rising and swallowing these cities, one foot at a time. The incremental nature of this crisis has seduced many of the world's leaders and policy makers that this issue can be held off without real and immediate action. They have so far failed to recognize the systemic repercussions the death of these coastal cities will bring. Issues such as domestic and global economic collapse, rising refugee crises, civil unrest, and upheaval of the world as we know it are a sampling of what is to come as many of the world's leading cities literally sink below the surface of the sea.

Like an annual event, the Atlantic hurricane season unfolds every year and we find ourselves watching live camera footage on the streets of some Florida city under water as the next big storm approaches. These flooding events are not isolated to hurricanes any longer. Many experts on the erosions of the world's coastlines have referred to the city of Miami specifically as America's "ground zero" in facing the threat of rising sea levels. Flooding here is no longer news but a regular occurrence. A recent study by the National Oceanic and Atmospheric Administration (NOAA) recognized an average sea level height from 2012 to 2016 to be about 4 inches greater than what was recorded two decades earlier[1]. Four inches might seem like a mere adjustment to where we should lay our sunbathing towels on a Miami beach, but it actually translates to much more. Rising sea levels mean changing weather patterns, and previously routine storms have today become emergency events. Such storms have also been the pivot points for the waters' further encroachment onto Miami's dry land. Once the waters advance upon the shorelines during massive storms, they are not returning to their prior pre-storm levels when the storm clouds blow away.

Miami is currently spending more than $500 million in a plan to elevate roads, install pumps, revamp drainage systems and raise sea walls. This is all part of an effort to save a threatened $40 billion worth of real estate in a tourist hot spot[2]. Such shifts have reshaped the political and economic realities of Miami. The current mayor of the city came to office on a platform of plans and promises to save the city from what others have perceived as its inevitable demise. Migration out of Miami has increased 397% since 2010[3]. The only reason the city's population has held steady in spite of this mass exodus is that even while longtime residents of Miami are leaving for better opportunities and futures elsewhere, immigrants, mostly from Latin America, have replaced the departing residents, huddling together in the few cheap pockets of affordable housing. Rising waters have already changed the domestic realities of Miami, and this will continue into the near future.

Rising sea levels drastically affect ocean front property in the developed world – meaning high dollar and pristine properties. These are the places where vacation homes, luxury hotels and casinos are built, and they are sitting at the edge of a rising crisis, literally. When these cities sink, service sector economies sink with them. The first people to escape are those with the financial resources and wherewithal to do so. The last to leave are those who have nowhere else to go and no means by which to go. In other parts of the world we refer to such stranded people as displaced people and refugees.

According to Laura Parker of National Geographic, more than 90 coastal cities in the US are battling chronic flooding that has become so rampant that a measure of population flight has already ensued from these areas. "By the end of the century, chronic flooding will be occurring from Maine to Texas and along parts of the West Coast. It will affect as many as 670 coastal communities, including Cambridge, Massachusetts; Oakland, California; Miami and St. Petersburg, Florida; and four of the five boroughs of New York City. The magnitude of the coming calamity is so great, the ripple effects will reach far into the interior."[4]

In Annapolis, Maryland, home to the U.S. Naval Academy, the town and campus are currently flooded on average 40 times a year. A report in the Navy Times in 2016 noted that the Navy Station Norfolk in Virginia and 17 other U.S. military bases located on ocean front property are expecting hundreds of floods a year and to be mostly submerged by the year 2100. That puts 128 military bases and over $100 billion defense dollars at risk of being under water over the course of the next few decades[5].

Scientists say that sea level rise on the east coast was less than 3 millimeters for the total time spanning between 0 to 1800AD. Then things shifted dramatically. Currently the rate of sea level rise is at 1.7 millimeters per year, the fastest rate in the last 2,000 years. In New York City, that rate has increased to 3 millimeters per year[6].

In 2017, Zillow, a national real estate firm, advised that the current value of all homes under threat from a rise in sea levels by the year 2100 amount to over $882 billion in real estate assets. Across Florida, 1 in 8 properties are at risk of being underwater during this time period. In Hawaii, the number is 1 in 10 homes, in Boston it is 1 in 6 homes, and the national total is over 1.9 million homes - roughly 2% of American houses[7]. This shift in the American real estate market, the foundation of the American economy, the American dream and the American middle class will be devastating. When real estate values fall along the coastlines with these sinking cities, it will not happen in a vacuum. Unemployment will rise, net worth will sink, populations will shift, frustration and disgruntlement will migrate, and America's domestic reality will radically transform.

Remember, It's Not Just Climate Change

The causes behind the rising seas are not uniform across the world. In some locations it is the result of melting ice in the arctic. In others it is thermal expansion in warming ocean waters or the movement of local ocean currents. In Louisiana, technology and infrastructure built in recent centuries to reduce flooding risks along the Mississippi River have had the unintended consequence of preventing the flow of sediment deposits down the mighty Mississippi that previously worked to strengthen the coastal zones. This resulted in massive soil erosion. Adding to this, oil and natural gas drilling in the area since 1901 further weakened the soil, causing portions of the state to literally sink even as local sea levels are rising four times faster than the global average.

Louisiana's struggles with rising sea level top all of what is taking place in the United States. Between 1932 and 2010, 80% of America's coastal erosion occurred in Louisiana as 1,800 square miles of land disappeared under rising waters. Major storms like Hurricane Katrina in 2005 have added to the severity and drama in the southern state. Between 2004 and 2008, Louisiana lost more than 300 square miles to the ocean[8]. The deepening crisis in Louisiana has wrought everything from economic to social upheaval in the state and surrounding regions.

After Hurricane Katrina, the population of New Orleans alone dropped by over 50% as 250,000 people fled the city. While the sight of parking lots full of FEMA trailers captured the popular media's imagination, these hurricane refugees spread to surrounding cities and states, inundating unsuspecting population centers with lives that had been ransacked by the hurricane. Rising crime rates and unemployment came with many of these refugees. More than $120 billion in federal spending was directed to the hurricane-stricken city. Sixty percent of this went to emergency relief instead of rebuilding. Total losses from Katrina in the Gulf Coast rose to more than $130 billion, with insurance covering less than $30 billion[9]. The simple fact is that many Gulf Coast residents never recovered from the great storm, and they serve as an example of what is to come.

A Global Concern and Paralysis

The crisis is not limited to the United States. In Rio de Janeiro, Brazil, recent storm surges have torn apart paved paths at the ocean's edge and caused landslides at popular cliffs that overlooked the ocean. Experts have warned that the rising of average global temperatures by only 2 degrees would decimate the city as rising sea waters would merge with surrounding lagoons to compound flooding.

Shanghai, China is considered the most at-risk city in the world when it comes to rising seas. It is one of the busiest port cities in the world and borders both the ocean and the Yangtze and Huangpu Rivers. As many as 17.5 million residents of the city are at risk of being displaced by flooding if current trends continue. As a result, the Chinese government has embarked on massive infrastructure projects including the erection of stronger sea walls, greater and more elaborate drainage systems, and building new dams.

Osaka, Japan, The Hague in the Netherlands, Alexandria, Egypt; the list goes on of major cities throughout the world who are being forced, or will soon be forced, to contend with the realities of rising sea levels. The greatest obstacle to the governments and leaders seeking to head off these future crises is not a lack of technology or expertise but convincing their own citizens that the gradual rise in surrounding sea waters is a significant threat that must be acted upon now. Although the advice of leading scientists and engineers is readily available to warn and prevent these unfolding crises today, the very gradual nature of the crisis itself tends to paralyze the hands of preparation and prevention until it is too late.

A 2013 report from a team of World Bank economists[10] suggested the costs of flooding around the world will soon rise to $1 trillion a year if steps are not taken to the mitigate the risks of rising sea levels.

"In terms of the overall cost of damage, the cities at the greatest risk are: 1) Guangzhou, 2) Miami, 3) New York, 4) New Orleans, 5)

Mumbai, 6) Nagoya, 7) Tampa, 8) Boston, 9) Shenzen, and 10) Osaka. The top four cities alone account for 43% of the forecast total global losses."

This list represents nations of the more affluent and developed world. Risks are even higher in the developing world where this crisis will take a greater toll on GDP, and there will be potentially more widespread tragedy due to the limited ability of poorer nations to respond to crises when they finally hit. The top 10 most vulnerable cities, when sorted by the potential risks calculated as a percentage of the nation's GDP, include:

- 1. Guangzhou
- 2. New Orleans
- 3. Guayaquil
- 4. Ho Chi Minh City
- 5. Abidjan
- 6. Zhanjiang
- 7. Mumbai
- 8. Khulna
- 9. Palembang
- 10. Shenzhen

REMEMBER the names of these cities. They will be featured in the headlines of the news stories in the coming years. This is where homes and businesses will be sinking. It is where the next generation of refugees will be fleeing from and seeking new lives, jobs, and homes. The locations they flee to will likely be the hot spots of new political debates, protests and extreme social polarization.

1. **Bum, Philip.** Flooding in Miami is no longer news — but it's certainly newsworthy. *Washington Post.* [Online] August 4, 2017. [Cited: February 28, 2018.] https://www.washingtonpost.com/news/politics/wp/2017/08/04/flooding-in-miami-is-no-longer-news-but-its-certainly-newsworthy/?utm_term=.e249527e31ee.
2. **Brasilero, Adriana.** In Miami, battling sea level rise may mean surrendering

land. *Reuters.* [Online] July 20, 2017. [Cited: February 28, 2018.] https://www.reuters.com/article/us-miami-sealevelrise/in-miami-battling-sea-level-rise-may-mean-surrendering-land-idUSKBN1A601L.

3. **NEHAMAS, ANDRES VIGLUCCI AND NICHOLAS.** Miami real estate is so expensive that locals are moving out. *Miami Herald.* [Online] March 23, 2017. [Cited: February 28, 2018.] http://www.miamiherald.com/news/local/community/miami-dade/article140447978.html.

4. **Parker, Laura.** Sea Level Rise Will Flood Hundreds of Cities in the Near Future. *National Geographic.* [Online] July 12, 2017. [Cited: February 28, 2018.] https://news.nationalgeographic.com/2017/07/sea-level-rise-flood-global-warming-science/.

5. **Myers, Meghann.** Rising oceans threaten to submerge 128 military bases: report. *Navy Times.* [Online] June 29, 2016. [Cited: February 28, 2018.] https://www.navytimes.com/news/your-navy/2016/07/29/rising-oceans-threaten-to-submerge-128-military-bases-report/.

6. **Homeland Security News Wire.** Sea-level rise accelerating along U.S. East Coast. *Homeland Security News Wire.* [Online] August 18, 2017. [Cited: February 28, 2018.] http://www.homelandsecuritynewswire.com/dr20170818-sealevel-rise-accelerating-along-u-s-east-coast.

7. **Rao, Krishna.** Climate Change and Housing: Will a Rising Tide Sink All Homes? *Zillow.com.* [Online] June 2, 2017. [Cited: February 28, 2018.] https://www.zillow.com/research/climate-change-underwater-homes-12890/.

8. *Louisiana fights the sea, and loses .* [Online] August 26, 2017. [Cited: February 28, 2018.] https://www.economist.com/news/united-states/21727099-has-lessons-americas-climate-change-policy-louisiana-fights-sea-and-loses.

9. **The Data Center.** Facts for Features: Katrina Impact . *The Data Center.* [Online] August 26, 2016. [Cited: February 28, 2018.] https://www.datacenterresearch.org/data-resources/katrina/facts-for-impact/.

10. **Duc, Tran Viet.** Which Coastal Cities Are at Highest Risk of Damaging Floods? New Study Crunches the Numbers. *World Bank.* [Online] World Bank, August 19, 2013. [Cited: February 28, 2018.] http://www.worldbank.org/en/news/feature/2013/08/19/coastal-cities-at-highest-risk-floods.

21

DYING OF THIRST

E ven while many parts of the world are sitting at the edge of crisis as leading cities and population centers are overcome with flooding, far more parts of the world are confronted with an opposite reality: there is not enough water. That reality is one of inequality and disproportional access. While New Orleans, Miami, and Shanghai face the threat of drowning, Cape Town and Damascus are confronted with a lack water to meet the basic standards of life for their own populations. One side suffers by drowning; the other side suffers by drought.

A United Nations study projected that as many as 30 nations – not cities, but nations – will be water scarce by the year 2025. Eighteen of these nations are located in the Middle East and North Africa[1]. Israeli water experts anticipate that half of the world will live in countries with chronic water shortages by 2050[2]. The threat of global water scarcity is not a future and far off threat. It is already happening. These experts are merely forecasting the rate at which this dire crisis will continue to unfold in the coming years and decades.

In 2008, Spain reported its national reservoirs were at half capacity even before the driest and hottest months of summer had arrived. Swimming pools sat empty. Beachside showers were turned off. In Barcelona, the region hardest hit by the drought, reservoirs were as low as 25 percent of normal operating capacity. Authorities reported that a "water war" had broken out between different regions of the country contesting for much needed resources. Tankers were being used to ship water into the thirsty nation throughout the year [3].

In 2015, Sao Paulo, Brazil's water reservoirs were operating at 12 percent of capacity. Large parts of the reservoir's surface were simply mud. At 20 million people, Sao Paulo is the largest city in the western hemisphere. Many of its residents were experiencing 12-hour water cut offs. The rich purchased water from outside sources and built water tanks. The poor waited for the government to resolve the crisis; and when the government failed to do so, they protested. Once again, this is not simply a story of climate change. Brazil holds 12-16% of the world's fresh water, more than any nation on the planet. Unfortunately, through government corruption and dysfunction, much of that fresh water is either polluted or simply incapable of reaching the nation's largest population centers like Sao Paulo[4].

Similarly, in Jakarta, Indonesia the issue is not a lack of fresh water. The city has an abundance of rains and rivers. It is frequently soaked in torrential rain and rising ocean waters but is still running out of potable water. Decades of corrupt and incompetent leadership have ignored the fact that the city is sinking below sea level. Infrastructure was not built properly. Fresh water resources now mix with sewage in an asphalt jungle of development focused on short-term gains at the expense of a long-term crisis. The balances owed on those past transactions are now coming due and the city's more than 10 million residents are paying the price. Portions of the city are now being literally abandoned because they are unlivable. The water crisis combined with anger toward government dysfunction and corruption has helped fuel extremism and violence throughout Indonesia. Against the backdrop of this crisis, the country is host to the largest percentage of Muslim citizens in the world. Pockets of this angry and frustrated citizenry are increasingly moving toward violence through various Islamic extremist groups popping up across the country. Indonesia was one of the world's largest suppliers of soldiers to the Islamic State in 2018.

In this way, a loop of failure has been established in Indonesia that is frequently duplicated in other locations around the world. Incompetent and corrupt governance brings forth dysfunctional and broken social systems and structures. These feed into a frustrated and angry populace who gradually move toward extremism. The extremists then retaliate against the government, tying its hands so that even if reforms were possible and within the will and desire of the government, cycles of impotence and dysfunctionality have already become the established norm.

Jordan holds the undesired potential of becoming the first nation – not city or province, but nation - to run out of water. The Jordan River is the country's lone water supply and it sits polluted and depleted; some of its aquifers have been pumped beyond repair. Sitting between Israel and much of the Middle East, Jordan has been a popular target destination for various refugee populations in the region for more than half a century. As a result, the population of Jordan has grown decade by decade even as the rains, already sparse, have declined. The population is too large and too poor for the country to afford importing water like others in the world have done, and the water shortages have already produced clashes between native born citizens of Jordan and the refugee populations.

The country has a fertility rate of 3.38, among the highest in the region, but this is dwarfed by the influx of refugees. Jordan was expected to have population growth of up to 9 million by the year 2035; but thanks to the wars and flight of citizens from Iraq and Syria in the last decade, that target was already hit by 2015. This forced a scramble for water resources in the nation. According to Maysoon Zoubi, head of the Higher Population Council and former Secretary General of the Ministry of Water and Irrigation, ten of the country's 12 aquifers are almost depleted now. In some locations, authorities are drilling more than a mile below the earth's surface in search of water. Jordanian citizens already have one of the lowest water consumption rates in the world: about 3% of what the average American intakes per year. It is only going to get worse. Weather patterns suggest less, not more rain for the next few years and extending for decades. Even before this, however, Jordan was never able to fill its water reservoirs[5].

In India, groundwater withdrawals have increased tenfold since the 1950s. In 2016 the New York Times editorial board noted how some 330 million people, one quarter of India's population, were suffering under the weight of a drought that was devastating the agricultural sector. Farmers were being forced from their lands. Power plants driven by water were being shut down. Armed guards were set up to guard dams and other waterways to prevent farmers from stealing water[6]. Only 17 percent of India's farms have access to surface irrigation projects. Most of the farmers rely on rains or pump their water supply from underground. This has resulted in a significant drop to the water supply throughout India. The government reports that water supplies have dropped across the nation an average of 47 percent in the last decade[7]. Half of India's national economy relies upon farming. As we saw in the previous chapters, when these systemic failures set in a great toll is taken upon the farmers themselves. Many farmers have been forced to sell portions of their lands and become indebted with the remaining lands in an effort to produce a harvest in this increasingly unwinnable situation. When these efforts and solutions fail, suicide is a frequent response. There were over 12,000 suicides by landowning farmers and farm laborers in 2014, a slight increase over 2013. Many more who do not commit suicide in the face of their failed farming enterprise abandon their efforts and move to the already overburdened cities of India in search of work, food, and resource for their families. Tens of thousands of Indian farmers have made this trek in recent years, further exposing and worsening the problems of India's untenable water supply issues in its cities.

Reservoirs and rivers in India are running dry. Long trains can now be seen rushing carloads of water from one part of the subcontinent to another in an effort to fill the desperate supply vacuums. In government-organized and supplied water distribution points, many

Indians line up for hours at a time to receive a supply of water for their homes. Fights frequently break out.

North America has not escaped the sad list of water crises unfolding around the world today. Mexico City is recognized as a major disaster waiting to happen as the population overwhelms the water supply. A 2016 study warned that 10 percent of Mexicans ages 15-65 could eventually try to emigrate north to the U.S. due to rising temperatures, droughts, and flooding in their homeland[8]. This would put a strain of an additional several million people on the United States' already polarized and overburdened immigration system.

In the United States, the western U.S. has experienced ongoing droughts for years. In 2016 Lake Mead in Nevada, the largest reservoir in the United States in terms of capacity, shrunk to its lowest level ever. Lake Mead is a water resource that supplies over 25 million people in Nevada, Arizona, and California. Bans and water rationing were instituted in California. In 2009, a state law required a 20 percent per capita reduction in water use, but within 5 years, experts were saying this was still not enough to ward off the effects of drought and the state's diminishing water supply. The website droughtmonitor.dnl.edu, an initiative by the National Drought Mitigation Center, tracks the situation in California and throughout the United States and demonstrates that around 90 percent of the state is under nearly constant degrees of drought and these conditions can grow quite severe.

California is not exempt from the social repercussions of the water crisis being experienced in other parts of the world, and these are emphasized in the divide between rich and poor in the Golden State. In 2015, when the state's governor called for another 25 percent reduction in water usage, the luxurious southern California gated community of Rancho Santa Fe instead saw water consumption increase by 9 percent. Wealthy members of the community argued that if they could pay for the water they should be allowed to use as much as they want even if that use was simply to water their expansive lawns to maintain the aesthetic appeal of their ranches. One particular member of the community argued against the logic of the water bans by saying: "You could put 20 houses on my property, and they'd have families of at least four. In my house, there is (sic) only two of us. So they'd be using a hell of a lot more water than we're using."[9] Meanwhile, across the U.S. water bill rates have soared, increasing by 41 percent since 2010. If this trend continues, a recent report suggests that almost 36 percent of Americans, 40.9 million people, will be forced to choose between paying their water bill or paying for rent and groceries[10]. Even so, the sentiments expressed in Rancho Santa Fe are echoed by those from the current crisis in Cape Town, South Africa on the other side of the world as featured in an article in The Atlantic:

> Why should the wealthy, who pay the most in rates and taxes, effectively subsidize water consumption in poor communities and in the farmlands, while facing a curtailment of the services they effectively underwrite? And why should high-income, tourist-friendly neighborhoods like Mouille Point be forced to host potential desalination plants, noisy eyesores that could just as easily be set up in less "desirable" communities? On the flipside, as a township resident and reporter named Suné Payne put it: "If my household of nine can survive on less than 350 liters of water a day, why can't others?" In Cape Town, the poor have always faced water restrictions. "There used to be a name for it," remarked one activist. "Apartheid."[11]

Throughout other parts of the U.S. a contest for water resources is growing between farmers and bulging city populations. The Colorado River, for example, provides water to over 30 million people in the western United States. More than three quarters of the population in this region live in cities and that number is expected to increase by 10 million more people in the course of the next 30 years. These cities will hold thirsty people and thirsty industries, but in the state of Colorado alone 90 percent of the state's water supply is designated toward agriculture. By 2030 Colorado, famous for its snow-capped Rocky Mountains, is expected to have a major water shortfall.

An acre-foot of water is considered enough to supply a family of four over the course of a year. By 2030 Colorado anticipates a shortfall of 118,000 acre-feet relative to its own population[12].

The global water crisis does not respect the boundaries of nations or the sophistication of economies. It is global. It is growing. It is happening now!

---

1. Arsenault, Chris. Risk of water wars rises with scarcity. *Aljazeera.* [Online] August 26, 2012. [Cited: February 28, 2018.] https://www.aljazeera.com/indepth/features/2011/06/2011622193147231653.html.

2. Jaffe-Hoffman, Maayan. Ben-Gurion University Institute tackles water shortage, hygiene in developing countries . *Jewish News Service.* [Online] August 12, 2016. [Cited: Feburary 28, 2018.] http://archive.jns.org/latest-articles/2016/8/12/ben-gurion-university-institute-tackles-water-shortage-hygiene-in-developing-countries#.Wph2J5Pwa34=.

3. Keeley, Graham. Barcelona forced to import emergency water. *The Guardian.* [Online] May 14, 2008. [Cited: February 28, 2018.] https://www.theguardian.com/world/2008/may/14/spain.water.

4. Gerberg, Jon. A Megacity Without Water: São Paulo's Drought. *Time.* [Online] October 13, 2016. [Cited: February 28, 2018.] http://time.com/4054262/drought-brazil-video/.

5. Schwatzstein, Peter. WHAT WILL HAPPEN IF THE WORLD NO LONGER HAS WATER? *Newsweek.* [Online] November 22, 2017. [Cited: February 28, 2018.] http://www.newsweek.com/2017/12/01/what-happens-world-without-water-jordan-crisis-717365.html.

6. Editorial Board. India's Water Crisis. *New York Times.* [Online] May 3, 2016. [Cited: February 28, 2018.] https://www.nytimes.com/2016/05/04/opinion/indias-water-crisis.html

7. Lakshmi, Rama. More than 300 million Indians suffer from a crippling drought. *Washington Post.* [Online] May 4, 2016. [Cited: February 28, 2018.] https://www.washingtonpost.com/world/asia_pacific/more-than-300-million-indians-suffer-from-a-crippling-drought/2016/05/02/6bfa5a42-d504-4f69-93cd-6e8a07f09239_story.html?utm_term=.53e7900e37ba.

8. Kimmelman, Michael. Mexico City, Parched and Sinking, Faces a Water Crisis. *New York Times.* [Online] February 17, 2017. [Cited: February 28, 2018.] https://www.nytimes.com/interactive/2017/02/17/world/americas/mexico-city-sinking.html.

9. Kuznia, Rob. Rich Californians balk at limits: 'We're not all equal when it comes to water'. *Washington Post.* [Online] June 13, 2015. [Cited: February 28, 2018.] https://www.washingtonpost.com/national/rich-californians-youll-have-to-pry-the-hoses-from-our-cold-dead-hands/2015/06/13/fac6f998-0e39-11e5-9726-49d6fa26a8c6_story.html?utm_term=.be5b6cd27d86.

10. Mack EA, Wrase S. A Burgeoning Crisis? A Nationwide Assessment of the Geography of Water Affordability in the United States. *PLoS ONE.* [Online] 2017. [Cited: February 28, 2018.] https://doi.org/10.1371/journal.pone.0169488.

11. Poplak, Richard. What's Actually Behind Cape Town's Water Crisis. *The Atlantic.* [Online] February 15, 2018. [Cited: February 28, 2018.] https://www.theatlantic.com/international/archive/2018/02/cape-town-water-crisis/553076/.

12. MERCHANT, EMMA FOEHRINGER. The Rain Barrel Is Only the Beginning of the West's Water Wars. *The New Republic.* [Online] April 11, 2016. [Cited: February 28, 2018.] https://newrepublic.com/article/132478/rain-barrel-beginning-wests-water-wars.

22

DAY ZERO IN CAPE TOWN - A CASE STUDY

I n early 2018 the city of Cape Town, South Africa became prominently featured in the international media as the first major modern city to declare Day Zero -- the day this second largest city in one of Africa's largest economies expected to officially run out of water. Previously, South Africa was most famous for representing the S in the BRICS acronym (Brazil, Russia, India, China, South Africa) established by Goldman Sachs as a key location for investment. Now, the nation was known for Day Zero. It was planned for April 12, 2018 – not for some time in the far-off future. Brief rains in February extended the estimated arrival of Day Zero to May but the story was the same. Day Zero was coming! Cape Town, South Africa was about to become the first major city in the world to run out of water.

In preparation for this, and in an effort to delay the arrival of Day Zero, clean water was rationed. Residents of the city were restricted to roughly 13 gallons of water per day. This amount was expected to soon be cut in half. For the sake of perspective, we should recognize that it takes 3 to 5 gallons of water to simply flush a toilet. Cape Town citizens were encouraged, therefore, to not flush their toilets, shower less frequently, recycle cooking water, and to drink less. Some areas were exempt from the rationing system. Hospitals, industrial areas, and locations where population density combined with water rationing would cause a higher risk of disease were all given less stringent limits; but even these allowances had their own deadlines. The people of South Africa recognized that when the water was gone this zero-sum reality would not have many other options or alternatives.

Many observers in the western media framed this story in the lens of climate change, but that was only part of the story. Since the end of the apartheid era in the mid 1990s, the population of Cape Town nearly doubled, soaring from 2 million to around 4 million. While the population grew, the rain patterns remained inconsistent. The area entered into its fourth consecutive year of droughts. Such events are not unprecedented in South Africa's history, but this time the lack of rain and the rising demand for water among the growing population demonstrated the frailty of the system itself. Cape Town's water supply was heavily dependent upon stored water, and the growing population's demand in the face of droughts inevitably led to Day Zero. Reservoirs were drying up!

The proclamation of Day Zero affected different people and groups within Cape Town's populace differently. Politicians leveraged the crisis to stir up both unity for a collective cause as well as division to denounce their rivals. The city was run by the opposition Democratic Alliance party. The party's representatives pointed out that the ruling African National Congress (ANC) failed to deliver water to all municipalities as required by law. In late January 2018, a representative of the ANC said the Day Zero warning was an opposition gimmick to drum up a sense of "gloom and doom." They further suggested their own remedies to the crisis, including reductions in production by brewers and soft drink companies[1].

The division among politicians was predictable, but what about the societal response? Scientists and sociologists were watching along with the rest of the world. What would happen if the social contract was broken and people no longer trusted the government to solve this wide-ranging problem? What would happen if the people began to take matters into their own hands? This possibility was seen as likely -- and in fact was already occurring in some parts of Cape Town.

In a recent survey by the World Bank that reviewed 154 different countries, South Africa possesses one of the widest margins of economic disparity in the world. Ten percent of the country owns 90 percent of the wealth. This context has triggered a very disparate set of responses from the rich and the poor toward the water crisis. The poor had to wait on the government to find a solution and they constantly counted and measured areas where they could cut back on food or other items and save their money for the purchase of additional water. The rich were taking matters into their own hands. For $6,000 a borehole could be dug so that a family of means could attempt to tap into underwater reservoirs. For $2,000 another company sold a machine that claimed to turn moisture in the air into potable water. For $400 a vendor was selling unique washing machines that claimed to use smaller quantities of water. Some of the rich were ordering desalinization machines which convert saltwater into drinking water. Others were purchasing bottled water by the truckload, enough to fill a swimming pool, and keeping the supply in their private storage. As a result, bottled water was sold out for days at a time in the richer neighborhoods[2].

People and businesses looking to profit from the crisis aided in elevating the level of panic in the city. Their marketing efforts reminded potential customers that the government could not be trusted for solutions to the water crisis. These rising levels of panic and distrust in the establishment inevitably merged with resentment toward the wealthier classes who were storing up water supplies for their own families and loved ones. It is not difficult to see how a water crisis similar to that experienced in Cape Town could quickly escalate to widespread social unrest and upheaval. Additionally, a spike in food prices was predicted before the end of the year as the effects of less water took its toll on local farms that could no longer produce harvests at the rate consumers had grown accustomed to in prior years.

In the end, Day Zero was averted in Cape Town. The unprecedented conservation efforts combined with a return of the rains that had been missing for so long. In June 2018 Cape Town experienced its first average rainfall amounts in four years[3]. Day Zero did not come – yet. Cape Town was at the forefront of this water shortage crisis, but experts point out that this will not be the last major global city to experience the same predicament. This is a modern trend that is only increasing in its scale and frequency. And very soon, Day Zero will not be able to be delayed.

---

1. TORCHIA, CHRISTOPHER. Cape Town to Set up Disaster Operations HQ for Water Crisis. *US News and World Report.* [Online] January 28, 2018. [Cited: February 28, 2018.] https://www.usnews.com/news/world/articles/2018-01-28/cape-town-to-set-up-disaster-operations-hq-for-water-crisis.
2. Sieff, Kevin. Divided By Drought. *Washington Post.* [Online] February 23, 2018. [Cited: February 28, 2018.] https://www.washingtonpost.com/news/world/wp/2018/02/23/feature/as-cape-towns-water-runs-out-the-rich-drill-wells-the-poor-worry-about-eating/?utm_term=.7e74e136fc5d.
3. Alexander, Christian. Cape Town's 'Day Zero' Water Crisis, One Year Later. *City Lab.* [Online] April 12, 2019. [Cited: August 30 2019, 2019.] https://www.citylab.com/environment/2019/04/cape-town-water-conservation-south-africa-drought/587011/.

23

WE SAW THIS COMING

The rising threat of a global water crisis has not arrived as a surprise. For decades it has been predicted and anticipated both globally and locally. A 1990 article in the Cape Times anticipated that Cape Town, South Africa would run out of water "in 17 years."[1] Nevertheless, a desalinization plant in Mossell Bay was shelved in 2011 because the water was seen as too expensive in the eyes of Cape Town's leaders and officials[2]. The threat still seemed too far away a mere 7 years before Day Zero was declared.

Upmanu Lall, Director of the Columbia Water Center at Columbia University, stated in a recent interview that he did not see the current crisis as simply a result of climate change. "Worldwide, people have designed water systems so that the amount of water they store and release is based on the worst drought they have seen in that region. The problem is that the estimate may only be based on 10, 20, or 40 years of data. It's not enough. The variation and severity of droughts can vary somewhat cyclically, depending on El Niño and other longer-term cycles. Cape Town has seen three years, which are some of the driest at least in the last 60 years, but if you look at the longer record, this is not altogether a big surprise. The 1940s had a comparable drought as measured by the total shortage relative to the target supply."[3] Kevin Winter at the University of Cape Town expressed the problem plainly in an interview with the Council on Foreign Relations. "We'd always believed that climate change wouldn't be as rapid as this, that it wouldn't give us a shock like this." There was in fact a Western Cape Reconciliation Plan designed to stop the South African water crisis, but its first major initiative was not planned to take place until 2019 and was to last all the way to 2032[4]. In other words, the first major initiative of the water scarcity rescue plan was planned for the year after Day Zero was expected to happen.

Part of the crisis is the result of poor planning or poor implementation, even when the planning was done correctly. In the eastern United States, there are plans for how to respond to a severe drought, but these plans are limited. They only consider the history of local jurisdictions over a short span of time in order to make predictions about what the future holds for the local water supply. Even worse, these plans are not connected to surrounding jurisdictions. They are formatted in a vacuum, as if presuming when New York is in the midst of a water crisis, other locations on the eastern seaboard will not be. These plans are not only short term oriented but also hardly realistic in determining how the local jurisdiction could deal with and recover from a severe water crisis. Experts at the American Water Project report there is currently not a reasonable strategy to deal with diminishing water supplies and potential crises in the future.

As the drought in California has worsened, consideration has been given to desalinization plants. The process which takes sea water, extracts the salt and converts it into fresh water is a popular solution in Australia and Israel that is being tested. Unfortunately, it is also expensive. Clean water made available through a desalinization process costs around $2,000 per acre foot, five times more than the cost of fresh water from reservoirs and groundwater. This solution requires a lot of investment on the front end. Planners are concerned that once the desalinization plants are built, after the high cost has been invested into this solution, the droughts could pass and angry taxpayers would still be left holding the bill. This is what

happened in Australia. American politicians have learned from that
political misstep. Why pay the cost for a future social need with the
price of their present political careers?

One of the more innovative approaches to the crisis is being
tested in China with the nation's "sponge cities" initiative. China is
seeking to balance out the paradox of crises with some cities
drowning in water while others are melting into dust bowl-status.
The initiative is currently being tested in 30 Chinese cities, including
Shanghai. The objective is that by 2020, 80 percent of its urban areas
will reuse 70 percent of the excessive rainwater they are receiving.
This will be done by revamping the industrialized infrastructure of
the modern city. The current infrastructure, as we saw in Indonesia,
causes a double hit on the water supply. Not only does it increase
water consumption and pollution, but also it decreases water absorp-
tion. The sponge city initiative will work to restore permeable roads,
parks, rooftop gardens and green spaces in flood prone cities and
transfer these gains to cities lacking water[5].

Sponge cities represent an ingenious possibility that is being
tested in a smaller scale in Germany as well. In China, the proposal is
still far from implementation and even farther from proving successful. Unfortunately, most of the world does not possess the coordinated political will or resources to follow suit. This type of
dysfunctional reality includes, and is in fact specific to, the United
States along with the continent of Africa and the hardest hit areas of
Asia. More concerning is the reality that the world as a whole has
possibly already passed a tipping point in the global water crisis.

1. ISAACS, LISA. #WaterCrisis: 1990 article shows Day Zero plans should've
   began years ago. *Cape Times*. [Online] February 1, 2018. [Cited: February 2018,
   2018.]   https://www.iol.co.za/capetimes/news/watercrisis-1990-article-shows-
   day-zero-plans-shouldve-began-years-ago-13044464.
2. City Press. Top desalination plant virtually untapped . *News 24*. [Online] July
   7, 2013. [Cited: February 28, 2018.] https://www.news24.com/Archives/City-
   Press/Top-desalination-plant-virtually-untapped-20150430.
3. Fecht, Sarah. Cape Town Water Crisis Highlights a Worldwide Problem. *Earth
   Institute Columbia University*. [Online] February 9, 2018. [Cited: February 28,

2018.] http://blogs.ei.columbia.edu/2018/02/09/cape-town-water-crisis-worldwide-problem/.

4. Tavitian, Maral. Why Is Cape Town Drying Up? . *Council on Foreign Relations.* [Online] February 22, 2018. [Cited: February 28, 2018.] https://www.cfr.org/interview/why-cape-town-drying.

5. Khor, Martin. Create "Sponge Cities" to Tackle Worsening Floods . *Inter Press Service News Agecy.* [Online] January 31, 2018. [Cited: February 28, 2018.] http://www.ipsnews.net/2018/01/create-sponge-cities-tackle-worsening-floods.

24

IT IS ABOUT TO GET MUCH WORSE

Much of the world's fresh water supply is held in aquifers. Aquifers are rock below the earth's surface that water can permeate through. When many of us think of the world's supply of fresh water, we likely think of rivers and lakes, but in fact there are hundreds of times more fresh water below the surface of the earth within these aquifers. Throughout history mankind has drawn from aquifers to supply its water needs. The drilling of wells and the pumping of water to the earth's surface is essentially the technology of drawing upon the aquifers to provide humanity's needs. As human civilization has grown and cities have become more densely populated, the need for that groundwater has increased; as a result, the aquifers are shrinking. This would not be a problem if the water being taken from the aquifers was being replaced, but increasingly we are learning that we are taking the water faster than it can be replaced. This is specifically what the alarming 2015 report illustrated in the satellite imagery from NASA.

In 2015, Water Resources Research published its findings regarding the state of the world's groundwater. The study utilized satellite imagery to study the effects of the world's overuse of the planet's aquifers. The findings were frightening. Among the 37 largest aquifers throughout the world, 13 of them were being depleted with little to no recharging. Eight of the aquifers were classified as overstressed with nearly no natural replenishment while another five were classified as stressed or highly stressed – this meant they were being depleted but there was at least some level of water flowing back into them. The Arabian Aquifer system, the most overstressed aquifer in the world, is the source of water for more than 60 million people. Second to this is the Indus Basin Aquifer, located in northwestern India and Pakistan. Third is the Murzuk-Djado Basin in North Africa[1]. These three aquifer systems represent the most overstressed aquifer systems in the world and the primary water resource for increasingly strained and desperate populations numbering in the hundreds of millions to billions. When aquifers run low or dry, rivers, lakes, and other freshwater resources begin to dry up and the land accustomed to agricultural production ceases to be fruitful.

It is important to realize that when we think of water being extracted from aquifers, we should not think only of drinking water. A far higher proportion of the water is going to agricultural needs – our food and water systems are thereby connected. Another large portion is going to help with energy needs. The steam from heated water helps fuel many of the world's power plants. The drawing down of the earth's water resources is about far more than drinking eight cups of water a day. Two billion people around the globe rely on groundwater for their daily use. Much of that water is coming from the aquifers, but other resources such as rivers and lakes are also a key supplier of the world's freshwater needs. The problem is, similar to the aquifers, the supply of these natural resources is not keeping up with the demands of a growing global population.

In the last 50 years, water consumption around world has tripled. That growth in consumption is in line with the growth in the global population discussed in earlier chapter. As water consumption has increased, the rains have slowed. This is a problem all by itself; but consider what takes place when temperatures rise and the rains do not come. We grow thirsty. We drink more. And even as we drink more, so also do the farms and agricultural industries we rely upon to produce our food.

In the United States alone, freshwater is used primarily for irrigation and electric power plant cooling (77 percent), municipal and industrial uses (20 percent), and livestock and aquaculture purposes (3 percent)[2]. All of these areas are negatively affected by a rise in temperature and a slowdown of precipitation.

In 2015, more than 4 billion people around the world were experiencing water scarcity for at least one month of the year. That's more than two thirds of the world's population. Many of these were located in the American southwest in areas like Arizona, Nevada, southern California, Texas and New Mexico. Recently on a school trip to the American southwest with my children's high school we stopped at a tourist shop at an exit near the border between Arizona and New Mexico. We toured the Navajo gift shops and stores that were set up like a strip mall in this area that represents one of the highest poverty rates in the United States. At one shop I asked the salesclerk if there was a public restroom we could use. "No running water here sir," came the answer. "Not in any of these shops. Welcome to the desert. There's an outhouse in the alley behind the stores." This is normal life for these folks. A mere hundred feet in front of these waterless stores sets the I-40 interstate system that stretches from Barstow, California to North Carolina. Billions of dollars of American commerce and trade travels here. Increasingly that trade is being strained by a growing drought and water crisis. Water managers in the United States expect shortages in some portion of 40 states within the next decade. Meanwhile, these residents of the dried out American southwest were experiencing a predicament similar to those in the water scarce regions of Mexico, Nigeria, Pakistan and Bangladesh. More than half of the four billion people who experienced water scarcity for at least an entire month in the year 2015 lived in China and India[3].

What happens when the water starts running out? This is probably the most important question to be asking. This is not some distant future event on the horizon. It is already happening. In 2012, Adel Darwish, author of the book Water Wars: Coming Conflicts in the Middle East, predicted the next water war to break out would likely be in Yemen. In 2015 war broke out in Yemen. It has not been called a "Water War." It has been more frequently classified as a sectarian or even a regional conflict between Sunni and Shiite Muslims backed by the respective power brokers of Saudi Arabia and Iran. But what if the political lens we are seeing and interpreting these conflicts through is actually mistaken? What if we are actually already beginning to experience the onset of water wars in the same regions that also hold the most strained aquifers and water resource systems?

This is what we are experiencing. Although the current conflicts cannot be directly tied to drying and overstrained aquifers and fresh-water resources, we find commonalities in all of the areas identified as having the most stressed aquifers. Human conflict is erupting on the surface of the earth far above the emptying aquifers. Yemen is only one of those stories. The Democratic Republic of the Congo sits on an aquifer system that is losing water three times faster than studies previously calculated. There have been ongoing conflicts here since the mid 1990s. The Murzuk-Djado Basin is the second most stressed aquifer in the world. Consider the fighting and upheaval that has raged in the area of Northern Africa, which sits atop this drying water resource system, in the last decade. We have been taught to relate the fighting to collapsed dictatorships, Arab Spring, ISIS, Benghazi, and more, but literally beneath the surface of these lands of conflict are the more basic issues of a struggle for resources and survival.

Scholars are divided on whether or not water resource declines can result in conflict. Many point out there has not been a war waged directly over water resources for more than 4,500 years. This perspective oversimplifies the issue. While there may not have been many "water wars" in the last few millennia, there have been plenty of wars over resources, oppression, and injustices. When we recognize that water is only one of the basic needs of life necessary for human survival, it is easier to recognize that it may be only part of the picture that leads to a greater conflict. The Pentagon has called these types of issues a "threat multiplier" when considering how a reduction in basic life sustaining resources contributes to global security and the potential for warfare.

A Columbia University report found that "the risk of a low-level conflict escalating to a full-scale civil war approximately doubles the following year." [4] Translation: when rainfall decreases, risks of conflicts exploding into civil war increases. In an assessment of potential risks due to natural resource limitations, PricewaterhouseCoopers observed, "Just as war over fire sparked conflict among early prehistoric tribes, wars over water may result from current tensions over this resource in the next few years. The Near and Middle East are the zones where there is the greatest threat. Two-thirds of the water consumed in Israel comes from the occupied territories, while nearly half of the Israeli water installations are located in areas that were not part of it pre-1967."[5] The United Nations has suggested there are more than 300 potential conflicts worldwide related to water resources, including river borders and the drawing of water from lakes and aquifers.

The potential for this type of conflict is nothing new, but we have learned to take this basic resource for granted. We barely notice the difficulty of cooperation and agreement that exists between various nations competing for water resources on behalf of their growing populations. In the last 1200 years, the world's nations and peoples have signed more than 3,600 water related treaties and agreements, but as the global population has grown such treaties and cooperation has been strained. Since 1950 alone, the amount of renewable fresh water available in the world has decreased by 58 percent per person. As a result, one quarter of water related interactions within the geopolitical sphere in that same time period have been of a hostile nature [6].

---

1. Jet Propulsion Laboratory California Institute of Technology. Study: Third of Big Groundwater Basins in Distress. *Jet Propulsion Laboratory California Institute of Technology.* [Online] June 16, 2015. [Cited: February 28, 2018.] https://www.jpl.nasa.gov/news/news.php?feature=4626

2. Bradford, Nick. The Increasing Demand and Decreasing Supply of Water . *Natural Environmental Education Foundation.* [Online] March 21, 2017. [Cited: February 28, 2018.] https://www.neefusa.org/nature/water/increasing-demand-and-decreasing-supply-water.

3. Fleur, Nicholas St. Two Thirds of the World Faces Severe Water Shortages. [Online] February 12, 2016. [Cited: February 2018, 2018.] https://www.nytimes.com/2016/02/13/science/two-thirds-of-the-world-faces-severe-water-shortages.html.

4. KIMMELMAN, MICHAEL. Mexico City, Parched and Sinking, Faces a Water Crisis. *New York TImes.* [Online] February 17, 2017. [Cited: February 28, 2018.] https://www.nytimes.com/interactive/2017/02/17/world/americas/mexico-city-sinking.html.

5. Agence France Presse. Water, the Looming Source of World Conflict. *Global Policy Forum.* [Online] March 20, 2001. [Cited: February 28, 2018.] https://www.globalpolicy.org/component/content/article/198-natural-resources/40338.html.

6. Cook, Steven A. Is War About to Break Out in the Horn of Africa? Will the West Even Notice? *Council on Foreign Relations.* [Online] January 16, 2018. [Cited: February 28, 2018.] https://www.cfr.org/blog/war-about-break-out-horn-africa-will-west-even-notice.

25

THE COLLAPSING SYSTEM OF ORDER

Many are familiar with stories from ancient history that featured the Egyptian people with the Nile River in the background. In the story of the Exodus, Moses wrecked the Egyptian economy when he miraculously turned the Nile River to blood with the touch of his staff and announced God's will that Pharaoh let the Hebrew people go from bondage. In the days of Rome's ascent to regional dominance, Cleopatra and Marc Antony relied upon the Nile as Egypt's power base in their civil war against the Roman Emperor Octavian. The Battle of the Nile in 1798 was the sight of a famous contest between Napoleon and the British as the world thundered into the modern age. The Nile has been central in the stories of history as a subtle player in the outworking of global power struggles. This is no less true today.

Few nations rely so heavily on a single water source as the modern nation of Egypt relies upon the Nile. More than 90 percent of Egypt's water supply comes from the Nile. The farmers of Egypt depend upon the great river's annual flooding of its banks to water their crops in an area of the world where rains are less predictable. The bulk of the Egyptian population is located in the Nile River Valley, specifically because of their need for its fresh water. For all this dependence and centrality of resource, not to mention historical association with Egypt, geography has not deemed the Nile River as preeminently Egyptian. Around 60 percent of Egypt's Nile River waters actually originate in Ethiopia. These same sources also provide water to Sudan. Thus, we have three very thirsty and growing populations vying for the same water resource. As those populations have grown, the resource of the Nile River has become increasingly strained, and efforts to better manage (or control) the waters have been seriously considered and contended in recent decades.

Egypt has one of the lowest per capita shares of water in the world. Each Egyptian consumes about 660 cubic meters per year. Compare this to the per capita water consumption in the United States which is almost three times that amount. As we have already seen, the Egyptian population is expected to double in the next fifty years, which will result in significant water shortages anticipated as early as 2025[1].

Meanwhile, Ethiopia needs water too. Ethiopia hosts one of the least developed infrastructures in the world and a dam would help in providing access to electricity for 95 million Ethiopian citizens. But such a dam would greatly reduce Egypt's water supply and trigger the already anticipated shortages more quickly and violently. Ethiopia's vision of a dam on the Nile is not a new idea. In the 1950s, Egypt followed this same logic when the nation built its own Aswan Dam on the Nile. Ethiopia's claim to the water as a natural resource of its own is not at all without precedence. In the 1950s, other nations that believe they have a natural right and claim to the waters of the Nile today did not even exist. This would include Sudan. Why should Egypt be allowed to consume the bulk of the waters of the Nile above what is allowed for the people of Ethiopia or Sudan where the waters actually originate? The potential for conflict and regional war here is immense.

These kinds of questions and issues are a point of tension around the world today. The United States National Intelligence Estimate on Water asserts that nations whose geography places them in an "upstream" situation are more likely to use their position to coerce their neighbors and secure themselves in the very near future. Beyond the year 2022, as water scarcity increases, these type of situations "will likely increase the risk of instability and state failure, exacerbate regional tensions and distract countries from working with the United States on important policy objectives."[2] The World Resources Institute projects we are now facing a rapid rise in global water stress with 33 countries around the world expected to face extremely high stress levels by the year 2040. A study published at Oregon State University observed that over 1,400 new dams are currently under construction across the globe, and these are part of an increasing threat of "hydro-political strife" The diminishing supply of fresh water is creating hot spots around the world and the potential for increasing conflict as a result of this is expected over the next 15-30 years[3].

Around 261 of the world's rivers are shared by two or more countries. According to Steven A. Cook at the Council on Foreign Relations, these international watersheds account for about 60 percent of the world's freshwater supply and are home to approximately 40 percent of the world's people. Asia hosts 60 percent of the world's population but only 36 percent of the world's renewable fresh water. "China, India, Iran, and Pakistan are among the countries where a significant share of the irrigated land is now jeopardized by groundwater depletion, scarce river water, a fertility-sapping buildup of salts in the soil, or some combination of these factors. Groundwater depletion alone places 10 to 20 percent of grain production in both China and India at risk. Water tables are falling steadily in the North China Plain, which yields more than half of China's wheat and nearly one third of its corn, as well as in northwest India's Punjab, another major breadbasket."[4]

This is not simply an issue of people growing thirsty. To comprehend the gravity of the situation, we must recognize the scale and the nature of its impact. As nations lose access to fresh water, agricultural systems crumble. Farmers are driven to desperation and poverty. Concentrated population centers grow angry and fearful. Riots erupt.

Populations migrate and become refugees. Civil wars break out. National order disintegrates.

These things are already occurring!

In April 2017, riots broke out in Karachi, Pakistan as demonstrators chanted "Give us water!" as they clashed with police forces. The Yellow River in China, the Chao Phraya in Thailand: these waters are drying up and the result is more frequent and intense outbursts of violence. Such violence and outrage is not frequently linked to water shortages when covered by the world's media conglomerates. We hear about political issues. We hear about shouts for democracy and against corruption. We hear about climate change. We hear about possible revolution and the people standing up to tyranny. In many of these instances however, when we move beyond the politics and the popular narratives, we find swelling populations where the water and food systems are collapsing.

Iran has been the focus of a spike in protests since 2009. In the western media, specifically, these events are framed within the context of a need for democratic reforms and an outrage against corruption and tyranny. A more thorough examination of the facts, however, reveals much more taking shape here. Many parts of Iran that historically supported the nation's agriculture system have suffered from a drought that has endured for more than 15 years. Farms have dried up and withered away. As farmers left their livelihood, they and their families moved to the cities where they settled in as quiet but frustrated strangers in their new homes.

Claudia Sadoff, a water expert who prepared a report for the World Bank, explained how in Iran, "25 percent of the total water that is withdrawn from aquifers, rivers, and lakes exceeds the amount that can be replenished." Within the next 50 years, the aquifers that fuel almost half of Iran's provinces will be entirely depleted. Lakes are shrinking as dams have been constructed to divert water to the cities. Lake Urmia, which was once one of the largest saltwater lakes in the region, has shrunk by 90 percent since the 1970s[5]. As protesters have pushed through the streets of Tehran in recent years, the underlying issue has little to do with Islam, democracy or hijabs. It is about the basic needs of life that are drying up for this people.

THIS IS how the world ends. It is not some far off future or prediction. These realities are already unfolding today. Many people across the globe are already experiencing water and food scarcity. Civil wars and violent unrest are already convulsing against the systems of injustice that helped perpetrate this irreversible destruction of the systems needed to support human life. The lands of the have nots are rising up in violent opposition to strike out against the lands of the haves. Meanwhile, the regions of the haves are building the walls, locking the political gateways, and strengthening the security in their borders and systems against the growing global unrest which they do not fully understand.

As we move into the fifth and final part of this story, we will explore how, as these multiple crises of population, food, and water converge, not only will the chaos escalate in its severity and scale, but we will also finally understand the systemic barriers that have been erected to guarantee the coming apocalypse is irreversible. It was not purposeful. Mankind did not deliberately build a system destined to collapse. They were focused on their immediate needs and interests. But within those needs and interests, and within that seeds of that global system that was established to facilitate them, lay the inevitability of our own terrible and chaotic self-destruction.

---

1. Michael, Maggie. Dam upstream leaves Egypt fearing for its lifeline, the Nile. *Associated Press.* [Online] October 2, 2017. [Cited: February 28, 2018.] https://www.yahoo.com/news/dam-upstream-leaves-egypt-fearing-lifeline-nile-064403350.html.
2. Dunn, Gregory. Water Wars: A Surprisingly Rare Source of Conflict. *Harvard International Review.* [Online] November 20, 2013. [Cited: February 28, 2018.] http://hir.harvard.edu/article/?a=10414.
3. Floyd, Mark. New assessment identifies global hotspots for water conflict. *Oregon State University.* [Online] July 17, 2017. [Cited: February 28, 2018.] http://

today.oregonstate.edu/archives/2017/jul/new-assessment-identifies-global-hotspots-water-conflict.

4. City Press. Top desalination plant virtually untapped . *News 24.* [Online] July 7, 2013. [Cited: February 28, 2018.] https://www.news24.com/Archives/City-Press/Top-desalination-plant-virtually-untapped-20150430.

5. Sengupta, Somini. Warming, Water Crisis, Then Unrest: How Iran Fits an Alarming Pattern. *New York Times.* [Online] January 18, 2018. [Cited: February 28, 2018.] https://www.nytimes.com/2018/01/18/climate/water-iran.html.

PART V

THE WICKED SCHEMES
OF MAN

The LORD saw that human evil was growing more and more throughout the earth, with every inclination of people's thoughts becoming only evil on a continuous basis.
   ***Genesis 6:5* (International Standard Version)**

26

SYSTEMIC REALITY

To understand the chaos unfolding in the world today, we need to recognize there are layers to identifying the true reality of the crises being confronted. Terrorism, refugees, and political dysfunction, for example, are crises - but they are not actually the real issues at hand. The situations are deadly and traumatic to those impacted by them, but they are merely the symptoms of greater underlying problems. Our inability to get to the underlying root of these problems and their causes explains the chaos of our world. It is a world that has already crossed the threshold and is steadily moving toward the end. The crises that are most demanding of our attention represent the collapsing outer facades of a deeper architecture, long strained and decayed. As the chaos intensifies, the real issues will become increasingly difficult to see.

It is clear from the previous chapters that the world cannot go on for another fifty years. This not a doomsday prediction. It is a simple mathematical calculation. There is not enough space, food, or water to supply the growing demand of mankind *as things are currently structured*. There *is* enough space, food, and water across the planet, but the global system through which these resources are distributed guarantees great abundance for small portions of the world and deprives the rest of the world. *This* systemic reality means there is not enough space, food, or water to supply the growing demand of mankind. This system was not deliberately designed to impoverish specific areas of the planet. It was designed to secure the more powerful areas. The suffering and misery that resulted was an unintended consequence, a byproduct of the global order and stability that was established in the last hundred years. The underlying systemic global architecture is driving the crisis on each of these three fronts to a place of inevitable collapse and destruction. The chaos we are witnessing today is the result of these underlying systemic crises.

Among all three of the foundational crises we have observed in the pages of this book -- space, food, and water -- population may be the most subtle but is also the most daunting difficulty to confront and resolve. The global population is estimated to hit 10 billion people around the year 2050. The weight of these new and aging lives will not be upon the prosperous and developed nations of the earth. In almost every one of those nations, population growth is going backwards. The crisis will weigh upon the poorest and least powerful nations of the earth. That is where the collapse of human civilization is already beginning to occur as the systems of order and life begin to implode upon themselves under the strain of this population growth.

Meanwhile, transformation of the global food system would require massive economic overhauls around the globe - including a short-term loss for the entire planet as we restructure the global economy. To save the future we would need to deliberately sacrifice the gains and abundance of the present. We would need to accept the reality of a *lost generation* from an economic perspective. The global economic system many have grown accustomed to would need to be abolished and a new one capable of sustaining the future put in place. There are precedents for this type of activity occurring. The Great Depression and World War 2 were terrible global events that allowed the great powers to restructure and establish the modern economy. The most difficult parts of resolving the food crisis would be establishing a fair and equitable global economic system (which undergirds the food system). Such a system would need to be created through a cooperative effort of the entire planet's nations and leaders – not simply the most powerful nations and those whose agreement and buy-in they purchase. That feat would be a truly unprecedented miracle!

Such cooperation is not coming. In fact, the insecurity that is spreading across the planet as the weight of these crises grows heavier has already proven we can expect *less* cooperation, not more. That is human nature. Even the Great Depression and World War 2 were unexpected events that forced a realignment of the global system and order. They were not a result of cooperation but of isolation, dysfunction, and finally forcing the great powers to change the terms of the global economy if they were to survive. We may see similar unexpected events in the coming decades as these crises unfold, but they are not likely to end in the same spirit of a new great global order as happened after World War 2. We will examine why this is unlikely in a coming chapter, but simply put, the nations of the earth lack the leadership or institutional strength to facilitate such convictions, no matter how great the need.

One doesn't need to look far to see the implausibility of restructuring the food system. McDonalds is estimated to have served more than 300 billion burgers since its founding. Those burgers are not reaching the 20 million in danger of famine and starvation which the United Nations warned us about in 2017. This is an image of a wider systemic issue of disparity that defines the global food system today. It is not rational. It is not reasonable. It was made by the unique designs of powerful nations and men to protect and secure their own interests. The destruction and disparity that resulted was not intended but also not prioritized. To undo these designs would require a massive shift in the global order of power and interest. That is not going to happen. Therefore, the next three decades will see the ultimate undoing of this system. As the scale of those starving to death increases commensurate with those suffering from obesity, the systemic convulsion against this injustice will rattle across the globe in various ways. And like the population crisis noted above, this convulsion and rattling has already begun in many of the same areas of the globe.

Finally, the water crisis should be the easiest of the three crises we have looked at to resolve. One part of the world is parched and dry, draining its aquifers, and dying of thirst. Another part of the world is literally sinking in excesses water. The solution is simple. Move water from the abundant part of the planet to the scarcity part of the planet. Yes, there are costs involved for such action, but if the situation were so dire, would a resolution not be worth those costs?

As we discussed previously, China has experimented with a solution known as "sponge cities" where the infrastructures of cities which are experiencing excess rains are being refitted to channel water to cities that are parched and drying. In Israel they are investing in desalination plants to convert saltwater into fresh drinking water. This should be the beginning of our solutions to the water crisis. But in order for this to truly be a solution, China needs to cooperate by sending water to India, Pakistan and Afghanistan. Israel needs to cooperate with Jordan and Saudi Arabia to ship their desalinated water to their citizens. The current system of international order will not allow for such cooperation. Instead, if these steps were to take place, it would only be at the benefit of the nations who have resource and at the expense of the nations who do not have resource. This is the way the world works. And that is exactly the problem! That is why no solution will take place. By continuing to pursue this style of wicked scheming, and self-interested politics and international relations, the nations of the earth continue to emphasize the very unjust systemic architecture that is perpetuating the crises.

The underlying principle upon which the architecture of modern human civilization and global order is built is the principle of self-interest and division. We do not act for the benefit of one another but for the benefit of ourselves. Therefore, division is always inherent to our motives and actions. This is true at the individual level and it is true at the larger collective level of nations versus nations. As long as the principle of self-interest is present, any solution brought forth to stem crisis will ultimately fail.

27

A VERY HUMAN CATASTROPHE

T he very nature of the global system of government and economy that has guaranteed the prosperity and security for some is also perpetuating and exasperating the poverty and scarcity experienced by so many others. This could have been predicted. It is the inevitable result of a system built upon the motive of self-interest. Human civilization functions predictably when self-interest is allowed to operate freely.

Capitalism and democracy are the ruling philosophies of our modern age. In the evolution of human society and progress, these are the winners when it comes to governing systems. Much of the 20th century was spent in an epic struggle between these systems and Communism. By the end of that century, most of the Communist world had collapsed and was seeking the path of the capitalist and democratic societies. Fundamental to capitalism and democracy is the issue of self-interest. As they spread across the globe in the last hundred years, theorists for international relations and global affairs even recognized self-interest as the basis for a predictable and manageable global order. Human societies and their leaders will always act in their own interests. This is not because they lack empathy for the interests of their neighbors. It is because self-interest is rational. It is a posture that says I will not harm myself and I do not want to be harmed. When individuals are planning career paths, they are looking at self-interest. When governments and leaders are planning for war or the avoidance of war, they are looking at self-interest. What will benefit me the most? That is the path I will take. What will keep me and my people safe, secure, and provide the most powerful advantage for future decisions? That is the route I will take.

The economic philosopher Adam Smith articulated the modern concepts of capitalism which we rely upon today. In his historically significant book *The Wealth of Nations* he wrote:

> *It is not from the benevolence of the butcher, the brewer, or the baker, that we expect our dinner, but from their regard to their own interest. We address ourselves, not to their humanity, but to their self-love, and never talk to them of our own necessities but of their advantages.*

Self-interest makes us predictable to one another. In a perverse way it allows us to be dependent upon one another. I know the butcher will not stop selling meat because he needs the money, therefore I don't have to become a cattle farmer and can invest my life elsewhere. I am now dependent upon the butcher to act in his own self-interest. This reality scales all the way up to the nations of the earth and the way they make war, peace, trade, and economy. Democracy and capitalism have taught us that when we all act in our own interests, we are better off. In the 20th century, as the world system was being redesigned following two cataclysmic world wars, this sentiment was put even more bluntly. In a quote frequently attributed to Winston Churchill, Charles de Gaulle, and Henry Kissinger, we learned, "Nations don't have friends; they have interests." We do not act for the sake of what is good or right, but for what benefits our own interests.

I have noted in earlier parts of the book the dilemmas of Communism and socialism. Cooperation is not optional, and among the greatest crimes and brutalities of the 20th century, from the Great Leap Forward in China to the Killing Fields in Cambodia, individuals and the community both failed under these systems. The fact that these philosophies failed as functional economic and governing systems pale in the light of their inhumane records. Enforced communism fails. The philosophy of self-interest inherent to capitalism and democracy has certainly proven effective in building a powerful global system of economy and independence. But the thing that holds the systems of democracy and capitalism together also has flaws, and those flaws should have been recognized from the outset.

Under this more successful governing and economic philosophy, the thing that holds us together also keeps us permanently and constantly divided. In a system built on self-interest it is not difficult to see how one person could become more powerful than all the others. This is not necessarily a bad thing. As long as there is cooperation, all can benefit from the growth and focus of power. A rising tide lifts all boats. If one of the boats is bigger than the others, so be it. The problem occurs when the resources become scarce. In that scenario the person with all the power will maintain his power and security at the expense of the weaker parties around him. The seeds for division and destruction are deeply sown into the very system of self-interested cooperation that the global system has been established upon. When the going gets tough, self-interest means I will sacrifice all that *you* have to maintain all that *I* have. In a zero-sum game self-interest ends in isolation and individualism.

The Problem with Self-Interest

This is a significant problem. Human beings were never designed to function independently and alone. Self-interest inevitably drives us to that manner of life. Successful and quality human life and civilization is built upon cooperation and a level of community that subordinates self-interest to the needs of our neighbors and those around us. The poet John Donne considered this scalable reality of how the individual man and the nations work more than a hundred years before Adam Smith published *The Wealth of Nations*. Donne wrote:

No man is an island entire of itself; every man
  is a piece of the continent, a part of the main;
  if a clod be washed away by the sea, Europe
  is the less, as well as if a promontory were, as
  well as any manner of thy friends or of thine
  own were; any man's death diminishes me,
  because I am involved in mankind.
  And therefore never send to know for whom
  the bell tolls; it tolls for thee.

That sense of connectedness is ideal, but it is not how the world functions. That is why the world will soon cease to function. In times of prosperity we frequently speak and laud praise for things built upon ideals such as unity, benevolence, and humanitarianism. But we need only the slightest measure of crisis and such ideals are quickly subordinated to the higher priorities of self-interest, personal security, and power. In the mid 1990s after winning the Cold War, Americans were speaking of a new world order, the end of history, and a new age of democracy and freedom. In less than a decade, the conversation shifted to a war on terrorism, Patriot Act, Guantanamo, and enhanced interrogation techniques. The global system is built upon self-interest. This is what inspires our policies.

Through self-interest we are able to justify the injustice and inequities that persist in the global system. We build a tolerance for cruelty toward those who do not belong to us. We hear of what the refugees are going through. We see the impact of terrorism in other lands. We read about people starving to death. We see images of the parched lands suffering in the global water crisis. We don't like any of this, but at least it is not happening here. In the land of the free and the home of the brave we are neatly secured from the chaos. We lose our empathy and prove our disconnectedness from the wider world. John Donne was wrong. We are an island, entire of ourselves. The bell does not toll for us. The bell tolls for them. This is the reality of living as an individual in a system built upon self-interest.

Almost twenty years before he published *The Wealth of Nations,*

Adam Smith published another, less famous, book entitled, *The Theory of Moral Sentiments*. Smith was as much, or more, a student of human nature as he was of economics. Here he noted once again the strange course of self-interest that dominates humanity. [I have added the emphasis in this passage from *The Theory of Moral Sentiments*.]

> *Let us suppose that the great empire of China, with all its myriads of inhabitants, was suddenly swallowed up by an earthquake, and let us consider how a man of humanity in Europe, who had no sort of connection with that part of the world, would be affected upon receiving intelligence of this dreadful calamity. He would, I imagine, first of all, express very strongly his sorrow for the misfortune of that unhappy people, he would make many melancholy reflections upon the precariousness of human life, and the vanity of all the labours of man, which could thus be annihilated in a moment. He would too, perhaps, if he was a man of speculation, enter into many reasonings concerning the effects which this disaster might produce upon the commerce of Europe, and the trade and business of the world in general. And when all this fine philosophy was over, when all these humane sentiments had been once fairly expressed, he would pursue his business or his pleasure, take his repose or his diversion, with the same ease and tranquility, as if no such accident had happened. **The most frivolous disaster which could befall himself would occasion a more real disturbance. If he was to lose his little finger to-morrow, he would not sleep to-night; but, provided he never saw them, he will snore with the most profound security over the ruin of a hundred millions of his brethren, and the destruction of that immense multitude seems plainly an object less interesting to him, than this paltry misfortune of his own.***

Smith could have been describing our own day and age here. Self-interest makes us blind to the world around us and even blind to our own self-focus. As long as our own comfort is not disrupted, we are fine. That is why the world can burn all around us, but we do not recognize it is burning until the flames reach our door.

Beneath the various issues afflicting the globe today are fundamental issues of scarcity. The population-crisis-strained areas of the world are running out of space. In the food crisis, they are running out of food. In the water crisis, they are parched for thirst. Those humans suffering here are turning to various pathways of response to the dire emergency with which they are confronted. Their responses make up many of our headlines today. From the stories of failed states and civil wars to ethnic cleansing and massive displaced populations, the chaos of our world is not occurring separate from root causes. But even deeper than these root causes are the systemic realities that perpetuate them. The self-interest-based nature of the global system assures us that not only will these crises not be resolved, they will also worsen. Those with the power to effect change will not make steps toward change until it is too late and the crisis has reached their doorway. Self-interest paralyzes us in the face of spreading collapse within the global system.

We Are More Than Political Beings

We must also confront one final and vital lesson here. When we dig down to the true foundational nature of the chaos confronting our world, and arrive at the dysfunctional design of self-interest, we are identifying something that the news media and political leaders will never recognize. The ultimate cause of the chaos spreading throughout the world today is not about resources or geopolitics. It is not about Republican or Democrat, socialist or capitalist. At the end of the day, the issue driving the chaos of the world and assuring us that this is how the world ends is the human heart. It is the unregenerate human heart that puts the self-interest above all else when push comes to shove. It is the human heart that would rather live alone as an island than give up an inch of its island for the benefit of those on the other side of the world. Self-interest results in blindness until it is too late.

When we are looking at the human heart, we are, of course, looking at spiritual issues rather than geopolitical issues. Even in the very opening words of the Bible, we are warned of the wrongness and dysfunction that is inherent in a self-interested design of life.

It is not good for the man to be alone. **Genesis 2:18**

Before sin, before the curse, before everything went awry, God made it clear we are not to live independent, self-interested lives. That was never His design. Throughout the course of scripture, we see Him looking to build less self-interest and individualism and more interconnectedness and community. In the Old Testament, He is seeking to build a nation. In the New Testament, He is building a church, a unique priesthood, and a holy nation (1 Peter 2:9). The self-interest-based design of life does not work. It leads to failure. It is not congruent with the way God made us to live. It is dysfunctional. We are seeing the approach of the end of the world because the world has been built upon a human-generated design that cannot sustain human life. It has not been built upon a divinely-given pattern of otherness and connectedness.

28

CONTAGION

When we as Believers see a terrorist attack today, most of us do not think about self-interest or issues of the heart. We don't dig that deep. We see a terrible atrocity that defies explanation. That is what the world around us sees us as well. The inexplicable nature regarding so much of what we see around the world is a characterizing feature of a global system in collapse. If we were at war, we could explain what we are seeing through the framework of war. If we were in a global economic meltdown, we could gather perspective through that paradigm. But today there is no singular crisis capable of defining all that is occurring around the world. Thus, we have chaos. Chaos is disorienting. It is confusing. It is a fertile environment for deception and disillusionment. To that end, one of the key objectives of this book has been to explain the chaos so believers can know how to respond.

To explain the chaos, we might start with an event or issue we are observing, but that should by no means be the end of our observation. We must go deeper. We must get to the heart of the matter.

Above all else, guard your heart, for everything you do flows from it.
Proverbs 4:23

This verse offers unique insight into understanding the chaos of the world around us. When we see tragedy and tumult, in order to truly understand what is taking shape we need to look and find the state of the human heart in the matter. In this chapter, I hope to demonstrate how this is done. We will look at a handful of terrible issues contributing to the chaos around the globe today. Then we will look deeper to identify what is behind them. As a preface, it should be noted that each of these issues are significant factors in the spread of the crises affecting the world. These issues represent the channels by which the chaos is spreading from the most deeply strained parts of the world to the rest of the planet. No nation is an island unto itself, and no nation can quarantine itself from the contagion of chaos and crisis currently emerging across the globe. These issues frequently bleed over into one another, often compounding or multiplying the scale of chaos and tragedy.

Terrorism

There is no universally accepted definition for the word terrorism. This is peculiar because most of the world order is caught up in a war against terrorists and terrorism. The Chinese say the Uighur people are terrorists. The President of the Philippines, Rodrigo Duterte, says his political opponents and drug lords are terrorists. Syrian President Assad says the Syrian rebels are terrorists. The Saudis say the Yemeni Houthis are terrorists. Vladimir Putin says his opponents are terrorists. President Trump warns Americans that incoming immigrants might be terrorists. There are many political definitions for the word terrorist today because the terrorist is the universal enemy of the modern world. Whoever seeks to deconstruct our current order, according to most leaders today, is in one way or another a terrorist.

This might seem cynical to some, but it is the reality we are facing today. At the same time, we know all too well that terrorism is a very clear and present danger around the world. From Boko Haram, to ISIS, to White Nationalism, the threat and impact of terrorism is not decreasing. It is getting worse. According to some studies, the

number of deaths around the world from terrorist attacks has actually decreased in recent years. This statistic belies the fact that the
impact of terrorism is not based upon its death count. Terrorism's
effectiveness is based upon its infamy, its fear-factor. When we are
afraid to go to certain parts of the world or afraid to let them come to
us because of terrorism, it is working. In Afghanistan's recent elections, many Afghan citizens did not vote for fear of Taliban and ISIS
terrorist attacks at the polls. The same occurred in Iraq and locations
in central Africa. Terrorism is a powerful force for destruction, fear,
and chaos in our modern world order.

According to the 2018 Global Terrorism Index[1] maintained by the
Institute for Economics and Peace, Iraq, Afghanistan, and Nigeria
were the top three hottest spots in the world when it came to deadly
terrorist attacks. The same report ranked the deadliest attacks of the
prior year. Somalia was at the top of the list with the 2017 suicide
bomber attack on the Safari Hotel where 588 people were killed.
Egypt had the second deadliest single terrorist attack in 2017 when
more than 300 people were killed as terrorists opened fire outside the
al-Rawda Mosque.

In 2019, Sri Lanka entered the fray for deadly terrorist attacks. On
Easter Sunday, terrorists hit multiple churches in the island nation
south of India. Two hundred fifty-nine people were killed and more
than 500 injured in the bombings. In Mali throughout the spring and
summer months of 2019, multiple terrorist attacks resulted in
hundreds of deaths and massacres. Christians and churches were
specific targets. This was seen as spillover violence from the neighboring nation of Burkina Faso where similar events were transpiring.
In Christchurch, New Zealand, a terrorist live streamed his atrocities
as he killed more than 50 people at local mosques. During this same
summer the terrorist group known as Boko Haram celebrated the
tenth anniversary since its inception in Nigeria. Since 2009 Boko
Haram has spread beyond the borders of Nigeria and infected the
neighboring countries with its violence, triggering social and
economic upheaval along with more than 39,000 deaths.

In all this violence and chaos, we have various religions, political

ideologies, and motives. In the case of ISIS, to which many of these
terrorists attribute their loyalty and inspiration, the tactic appears to
be simply anarchy. They want to upend the system. They want to
destroy. At one time ISIS hoped to resurrect an Islamic Caliphate, but
today that goal is secondary to wanton destruction and the spread of
fear. Ultimately, this how we can define terrorism. It is too erratic to
be captured in a single ideology or political goal or tactic. Terrorism
is not about what is intended to be accomplished. Terrorism is about
contagion. It is a package through which the chaos, fear, and violence
of one area of the planet can be encased and spread to another area.
As it touches down in those other areas, it sets off ripples and
counter-effects that cause chaos to spread across the globe.

As ISIS grew in influence in the middle part of this decade, the
group's attacks began to hit lands far from the so-called caliphate's
borders. Attacks in Paris, Belgium, Canada, and Australia triggered
countereffect measures from these lands of liberal western democracies. The effects of terrorism and a growing refugee crisis (within
which many see terrorists hiding) have led to a resurgence of
rightwing nationalism in much of the western world. The politics of
many parts of Europe have been drastically reshaped in response to
the threat of terrorism.

It is easy to become overwhelmed by the fear tactics of terrorists.
That *is* the point of its effectiveness, after all. When we look more
objectively at the issue, however, we find some interesting observations. In nearly every nation where terrorism thrives as a legitimate
and constant threat, rather than a periodic anomaly, the issues of
population, food and water are underlying factors shaping the political and social realities of these nations. In fact, when we review the
Global Terrorism Index of 2018, the top 19 nations impacted by
terrorism in 2017 all struggled with at least one level of crisis in these
basic global disasters. From Iraq (#1 on the list) to Kenya (#19 on the
list) issues of population growth, food shortages, and water crisis
were taking an unprecedented toll upon the societies where
terrorism is flourishing and having deep impacts.

We frequently look at terrorist activity in the aftermath of a senseless and brutal attack and are confounded by the irrational hatred and violence. Observing the issue from another perspective might help calibrate our understanding. In places where the population, food, and water crises weigh the heaviest, society and government are being pulled apart. Terrorism is one response to the perceived injustice being experienced by the people in these nations. As they strike out against the surrounding system, they are not looking for a political objective. They are looking for a sense of justice or perhaps just a sense of being heard. The system is collapsing, and they are caught as victims in the collapse. In their darkened minds the activity of terrorism at least gives them a voice to be heard through. As the world sinks all around them, they will take others down with them in a fit of rage.

The population, food, and water crises are not entirely causing terrorism, but there is definite evidence of a correlation. As life gets more difficult in the areas of the earth hardest hit by these crises, terrorist activity and brutality intensify. Terrorism spreads the chaos inspired by these issues. Boko Haram was born in the areas of Nigeria suffering most under the weight of poverty and food scarcity. Their terrorist activity packed the chaos and unleashed it into the more prosperous areas of Nigeria and the surrounding nations. The whole world is now aware of Boko Haram even if it is unfamiliar with the organization's genesis and the issues that led to its rise.

It is a stretch to say that issues of population, food, and water are the cause of terrorism, but if we subtract these issues from the equation, we certainly see an impact in the scale of terrorist activity. This observation leads us to a deeper recognition. Terrorist motivations and violence spring from a darkened human heart. Individuals who transition from victims of societal collapse to psychopathic murderers bent on destruction of innocent lives should not be pitied, but there is a reason why they have made this move toward darkness. Proverbs 13:12 explains, "Hope deferred makes the heart sick..." There are few things that epitomize a sickened heart more than an individual willingly and deliberately murdering innocent lives. In the case of terrorist activity, we can also add the suicidal element of these murders. It is not a rational act. It is not a political act. It is a depraved act of a sickened heart. To understand the chaos of the world around us we should recognize the elimination of hope that urged that heart towards its sickened state.

The global crises of population, food, and water are wrecking nations and societies. As these systems unravel, individual lives are caught in the collapsing state of affairs. As people surrender hope, their hearts darken and grow sick. We do not have to imagine the measure of their hopelessness and darkened and sickened hearts. We see it in the headlines every day.

Refugees

Following World War 2, the globe saw a massive refugee crisis. This crisis was brought on by the devastation of Europe during the war and the end of colonialism throughout Asia. This refugee crisis, apparent in lands from China to India, Pakistan to Israel, and to much of Eastern Europe, was the primary focus of the newly formed United Nations after World War 2. The world had never witnessed such global devastation as the war brought. On top of that, the collapse of the colonial system and the birth of new and independent nations in many parts of the world meant massive population transfers or displaced peoples. Many of the Palestinian people still live in refugee camps today. One third of the Palestinian refugee population today, 1.5 million people, still live in refugee camps in Lebanon, Jordan, Syria, and the Occupied Territories of Israel[2].

This historical refugee crisis in the postwar years was unlike anything the world had seen, because World War 2 was unlike anything the world had seen. But it was explainable. It made sense. There was a refugee crisis in India and Pakistan because of the effects of the partition of these two nations and their newly established independent states. It was not a good thing. It was a tragedy. But it was explainable. There was a refugee crisis in Eastern Europe because of the combined Soviet and Nazi Germany atrocities and destructions that had been unleashed there. It was barbaric. It was tragic. But it was explainable.

Today we hear of the modern refugee crisis and it is explained as the worst we have witnessed in more than half a century. The baseline that is being referenced here is what occurred throughout the world after World War 2. We are witnessing and experiencing the greatest refugee crisis in the history of the world since World War 2. But there is no World War that produced our current crisis. There is no collapsing colonial system. It is tragic but far less explainable than what was observed after World War 2.

According to the United Nations Refugee Agency[3], "We are now witnessing the highest levels of displacement on record." More than 70.8 million have been forced from their homes worldwide. Among this number are more than 40 million people classified as internally displaced. These are those who have lost their homes by war and violence but still remain within the borders of their home nations. Included in the count of internally displaced people would be many of the citizens of Syria, Afghanistan, Yemen, and other war-torn countries who lack the resources to flee to another country. Another 25.9 million people are classified as refugees. More than half of these are children under the age of 18. Every two seconds a person is forcibly displaced as a result of violence or persecution, and the total of displaced peoples across the world keeps growing. These are the people we frequently see fleeing across the Mediterranean from North Africa or the Middle East, hoping to find sanctuary on European soils. More frequently, we do not see them at all. The refugee population has become fertile ground for a revived slave trade and sex trafficking.

While the European refugee crisis receives a lot of attention in the international media, it is not really a large part of the global refugee and displaced persons crisis. In 2017 Lebanon hosted the world's largest refugee population. These are people who have fled from conflicts in Syria and Iraq. One in six people in Lebanon were refugees. That number does not include the Palestinians. In Jordan, 1 in 14 people were refugees. In Turkey the number was one in 23. [4]

Many of us might recognize the war in Syria as a cause for this booming refugee crisis, but Syria was not even the leading nation contributing to the human flow of refugees. In 2017, South Sudan ranked ahead of Syria when more than a million people fled their homes that year. Included in the top six nations where the populations were fleeing were Myanmar, Burundi, Democratic Republic of the Congo and the Central African Republic – all hosts to crises that received very little attention in the international media. In 2019, Venezuelans became one of the largest displaced people groups in the world. More than 4 million Venezuelans fled the country between 2015 and 2019[5].

Once again, we see a correlation of the refugee crisis to the core crises afflicting the earth that we have observed in earlier chapters. In nations where the refugee and displaced persons populations are bursting, population, food, and water crises are significant. We observed some of these in our case studies earlier in the pages of this book. War and violence are frequently also correlated to the flight of refugee populations from their homelands; but beneath the war and violent upheaval we find foundational systemic collapse. Excess population booms along with food and water scarcity are common factors in the war-ravaged lands producing the bulk of the modern displaced persons crisis. And once again, this crisis is operating as a distribution system to spread the chaos from one part of the world to other parts of the world. The leading hosts for these displaced populations are not European nations, but nations that border the core crisis nations.

These nations receiving the refugees are the leading recipients of international aid toward the refugee crisis, but the aid isn't enough. They are also suffering under the weight of population, food, and water crises. We can see the ripple effects playing out. A national crisis in Syria spreads to become a regional crisis in the Middle East. This spreads to a global crisis as the effects and counter effects compound onto one another. We have seen the impact of the global refugee crisis upon the nations of Europe and the United States even though these domains are nowhere near the leading sanctuaries for fleeing refugee families. All of these issues combined become the explanation for the chaos all around us. It is layered and more complex than the popular political narratives frequently lead us to believe, but all more apparent and devastating to the global system than many realize.

And beneath the crisis is the spiritual reality. The way in which societies and social systems are to work has been violated. Scripture clearly lays out principles and standards upon which the God-ordained design for societies and nations should operate when we confront refugees. In the Old Testament, foreigners were to be treated as native citizens.

> *The foreigners residing among you must be treated as native-born. Love them as yourself, for you were foreigners in Egypt. I am the Lord your God. Exodus 19:34*

They were to be included in the social apparatus of the nation founded upon God's word. (Deuteronomy 16:14, 26:11) Special accommodations were to be made to support and aid foreign refugees. (Leviticus 23:22, 25:35; Deuteronomy 14:28-29) Jesus spoke of our care for the strangers in Matthew 25, *Whatever you do to the least of these, you do to me.* Further, scripture is also very clear about how we should regard the significant proportion of refugees today who are children, orphans, and widows.

> *Religion that God our Father accepts as pure and faultless is this: to look after orphans and widows in their distress and to keep oneself from being polluted by the world. James 1:27*

There *is* a social standard upon which humanity is to be built. That standard is the prescription of God. When we see societies and nations imploding and spreading that implosion to other nations and parts of the world, we will always see a violation of His standard. The design of God does not guarantee that nations will be perfect or that the world systems will resolve the issue of refugees if they will abide by the written standards of God. But it does demonstrate how to prevent a contagion of the chaos. The massive depths to which we are sinking today when it comes to the global refugee crisis are evidence of a continued violation of the will of God in the earth.

The refugee crisis is a spreading chaos of global proportions. Beneath the chaos we see root causes of population, food, and water. And underneath these we see a growing crisis far out of line from the prescribed standards of God.

Failing States and Civil Wars

A delicate balance holds all of our systems and international order together. Imagine it like the solar system of the universe. Nothing exists in isolation. When one planet or star collapses, the whole system surrounding it is thrown into chaos and disorder by the effects of gravity. The degree of that chaos varies depending on how close you are to the collapse, but everything in the system is eventually impacted. Similarly, when a nation fails, the global order is jolted by the chaos. The balance is upended. The whole system of the global order is moved to counteract the loss of systemic balance. Frequently that movement results in further chaos itself.

One of the troubling trends of the 21st century is the rising number of failed states. We did not pay much attention to it when it occurred in prior decades because it was usually less about a state failing and more about a revolution or dramatic shift in government. That is not the case today. A former senior fellow at the Cato Institute noted, "The greatest threat to global security is the rapidly increasing number of failed states."[6] A failed state is simple to describe. It is a nation whose political or economic system has become so weak that the government is no longer in control. Into that vacuum rise terrorist organizations, civil wars, and the spread of chaos to the surrounding international order.

In 2005, the Fund for Peace and Foreign Policy Magazine began tracking the rising number of failed states around the world with its *Failed States Index,* later renamed the *Fragile State Index.* The higher a state sits on the index, the more vulnerable it is to failure. In 2018, the top ten most fragile states were:

- 1. **South Sudan**
- 2. **Somalia**
- 3. **Yemen**
- 4. **Syria**
- 5. **Central African Republic**
- 6. **Democratic Republic of Congo**
- 7. **Sudan**
- 8. **Chad**
- 9. **Afghanistan**
- 10. **Zimbabwe**

These are nations where the government cannot be counted upon to protect its people. They are nations where systems that the rest of the world takes for granted -- sanitation, healthcare, education -- are no longer operating in much of the country. They are also nations racked by terrorism, insurgencies, civil war, corruption, and despotism. They are falling apart, and in most ways, they are failed states.

Civil war is one of the most common symptoms of a failed state. In 2015, of the approximately 200 nations around the world, thirty were dealing with a civil war. Many of these wars included external parties in the fighting and violence, further complicating and escalating the violence and chaos. In 2017 political scientist Barbara F. Walter observed the significant increase in civil wars across the planet since the year 2000. She wrote for Political Violence @ a Glance that "civil wars have gotten longer, bloodier, and more numerous."

There are a variety of causes leading to this alarming rise in failed and divided states, but the causes frequently not mentioned are those we have covered in this book. Under the surface of every nation leading the fragile state index and almost every nation racked by civil war today are the crises of – you guessed it –population, food, and water. While academics note the rise of our interconnected world and communications leading to more civil wars and failed states, they overlook the obvious. We are witnessing the beginning of the end of the world. We are seeing whole states fail under the strain of collapsing foundational systems needed to uphold civilization. The chaos is spreading. At the dawn of civilization, humans banded together in the first cities and later in the first nation-states because this organizational method allowed for a more efficient method to gain security and distribute resources. Today that system is collapsing.

"Where there is no vision, the people are unrestrained, But happy is he who keeps the law."
Proverbs 29:18 NASB

The restraint and order that once held the globe together is being cast off today. People around the world have lost hope, have lost faith in their leaders, and in the system that was to secure and provide for them. They see the excess and corruption alongside poverty and misery. For many, more and more every year, there is no longer any reason to remain loyal to a global system that has been so treacherous toward them. The chaos we are witnessing around the world today is the collapse of a global order that is no longer trusted and no longer capable of restraining the people. The effects of the population, food, and water crises are rising to the surface at an accelerating pace. Even in the light of this understanding, however, we must see that the deeper root cause of the global chaos is a violation of fundamental spiritual principles and designs. The human heart is breaking as much as the global system -- and this explains the chaos all around us.

---

1. Institute for Economics and Peace. *Global Terrorism Index 2018 Measuring the Impact of Terrorism.* Sydney : Institute for Economics and Peace, 2018.
2. UNRWA. Palestine Refugees. *United Nations Relief and Works Agency.* [Online] https://www.unrwa.org/palestine-refugees.
3. Figures At A Glance. *UNHCR - The UN Refugee Agency.* [Online] June 19, 2019.

[Cited: August 28, 2019.] https://www.unhcr.org/en-us/figures-at-a-glance.html.

4. United Nations Refugee Agency. Global Trends Forced Displacement in 2017. *United Nations High Commissioner for Refugees.* [Online] [Cited: August 28, 2019.] https://www.unhcr.org/globaltrends2017/.

5. BBC. Venezuela crisis: Four million have fled the country, UN says. *BBC.* [Online] BBC, June 7, 2019. [Cited: August 28, 2019.] https://www.bbc.com/news/world-latin-america-48559739.

6. Rahn, Richard W. The Rise of the Failed States. *Cato Institute.* [Online] July 6, 2015. [Cited: August 29, 2019.] https://www.cato.org/publications/commentary/rise-failed-states.

29

LEADERLESS

I n the face of growing global chaos there are frequently two very different responses offered. These responses represent the fundamental political philosophies of the modern age. In the US we call them Democrats and Republicans; or liberals and conservatives. Around the world they go by different names, but still reflect the same standard political philosophies. The contest between these two philosophies has been the ongoing story of global politics for the last century.

One response suggests we can counter the growing chaos and its root causes through a belief in strong central authority and government. The other response believes the markets and "invisible hand" will bring about solutions. We simply need to stand back, make sure people are free, and they will find a solution to each problem on their own. (Everyone operates according to his or her self-interests, as you recall.) Each of these unique philosophies and approaches to the growing chaos of our times has its own list of successes and achievements that its proponents use to demonstrate their philosophy is best. Thanks to stronger governments and centralized authority, we have not had another great depression or world war for more than 70 years. Thanks to freedom and open markets, we landed on the moon and entered the tech age.

But as we have seen, specific implementations of these philosophies have demonstrated large-scale failure against the growing chaos. China and India utilized their strong central government authority and instituted historic moves to curb the population growth in their nations. China used the one child policy, making sure each home had only child – preferably male. India instituted sterilization, mostly among the poor, beginning in the 1970s. It is difficult to find a clearer demonstration of central government powers being utilized to combat the global population crisis. And yet for its entire dispassionate, objective, centralized approach to the issue, these strategies failed massively. China boasts the largest population in the world today, with a deficit of eligible single women to marry its high population of young single men born under the one child policy. Many of the families of these single men are turning to sex trafficking to guarantee a child and heir for their sons. The impoverished female sex slaves are discarded or placed back into the trafficking system after they have produced and heir for the Chinese males. India is expected to surpass China in the next few years to become even more populous. This is occurring even while the gap between rich and poor in India continues to strain its resources and social bonds. It is no coincidence that in the social and economic stress confronting India today, the majority of the nation's voters turned to a Hindu nationalist in the form of Narendra Modi in 2014. As the population and economic stress in India grows, so does insecurity among its Hindu majority.

On the other side of the equation, institutions like the World Bank and International Monetary Fund were developed to spread the values of free market capitalism and democracy around the world. This would insure the growth of freedom, innovation and prosperity. Instead, these institutions have empowered corruption and fostered a system where one part of the world is enriched at the expense of other parts of the world. Even after forty years of intervention from the World Bank there is a growing sense of devastating injustice felt in places like Egypt, as we saw in our case study on the global food crisis. The values and structures of the free market not only failed the people of Egypt and others – they betrayed the people who believed in them.

The failure of these philosophies is indicative of a wider failure of leadership in this season when the world needs the hand and voice of wise leaders more than ever. In the chaos of World War 2 and the Great Depression, men like Franklin Roosevelt, Winston Churchill, and Joseph Stalin arose to guide the world through the chaos and toward a new global system of order. They were not perfect men by any account. Stalin was an evil tyrant. But they guided the trust of their constituents through the chaos and to a safer and more secure world. Such leadership is not only absent today, but the conditions for leaders to arise appears utterly lost. There is no political savior coming to heal the chaos confronting the world today.

After the collapse of communism in the early 1990s, many believed we had entered a new era of peace, prosperity, and democracy. The political philosopher Francis Fukuyama explained in his book *The End of History and the Last Man* that liberal democracy was the final form of government, the apex of human civilization, and that the struggle of ideologies among civilizations was now at an end. He did not see the war on terror coming or what another political thinker, Samuel Huntington, called *The Clash of Civilizations*. Both political philosophers perceived liberal democracy as the height of human achievement. They did not foresee how democracy would be put on steroids with the advent of the World Wide Web or that the power of the individual, entitled voice would work to paralyze the global system of democracy.

The two leading historical cultures of democracy are the United States and the United Kingdom. Consider where they sit today. The UK is seeking a withdrawal from the interconnected global system of democracy by way of Brexit. Even in Brexit, the country is narrowly divided, and the tensions and polarizations of that divide have only escalated since the original vote in 2016. That same year, the US installed Donald Trump to the presidency. Some may argue about this man's qualifications and fitness for office, but few would suggest he represents an image of unity and strength in the American political system. The election of President Trump was about a hard shift in American politics, where division and polarization now became a permanent fixture of our political dialogue.

Around the world, the state of politics is also best classified in terms of dysfunction and division. Democracy, far from alleviating the pains and problems of the global system, has amplified the rate at which these modern political realities flow. This generation does not trust its leaders nor institutions, and that distrust has rattled the global order of politics into gridlock and deterioration.

Many of the issues we looked at in this book fall into the area of climate change and environmental concerns. As we observed in part one, however, that language cannot be used effectively today because Americans are divided on the subject. One group believes it is the most significant emergency confronting the world today. The other group is not even sure it's a real emergency or even a real issue. The lack of credibility in our leaders, our media, our experts, and our institutions all serve to push the adherents of opposing worldviews on this issue further and further apart. Meanwhile, the different political parties and candidates leverage this divide for their own interests by either perpetuating a belief in climate change as true science or the belief that the so-called science is merely political hocus pocus. Voters who oppose one side's perspective one the issue are demonized as fools and ideologues bent on conspiracy by the other side. Both sides are guilty of furthering the divide. No ground is gained on the issue, one way or the other. Dysfunction and polarized division accelerate in their extreme distrust of the *others*.

This is not only an American or western democracy phenomenon. In the Democratic Republic of the Congo, the second largest Ebola outbreak in history began in August 2018. The world attempted to respond through various institutions that were born to specifically address such a crisis. The World Health Organization and Doctors Without Borders sent teams and clinics into the interior of the DRC to help mitigate the growing crisis. Rather than welcoming the doctors and clinics, however, locals began attacking and burning down the treatment facilities. Doctors were literally killed in these attacks. This violence added to the spread of the outbreak, and it increased concern that a regional crisis would soon envelope the region. Why were the would-be recipients of medical aid attacking? They were attacking because they believed the doctors and international organizations, far from bringing them aid, were actually responsible for spreading the disease. A conspiracy was more believable than humanitarian aid to people who have served as the pawn of international political dramas and atrocities for more than a century.

Diseases once considered cured: measles, cholera, and malaria, are now making a comeback in war torn and poverty-stricken areas of the planet under these same conditions. From Haiti, to Yemen, to Afghanistan, locals believe the cures for the diseases are actually a front for institutions like the World Health Organization and the United Nations to infiltrate and corrupt their society. Why would they believe such a thing? Because in many instances, that was exactly what happened. The CIA used a fake vaccination drive to secure DNA samples from Osama Bin Laden's family in the war on terrorism[1]. United Nations aid workers dispatched to Yemen in 2018 became involved in an embezzlement and corruption scandal. In 2016, the Secretary General of the United Nations released a report confirming that a UN base in Haiti was the source for a cholera outbreak in the country[2].

Across the globe, as the crisis and spread of chaos intensifies, the only thing uniting the people of the world is a lack of trust in their government and leaders. In 2001, the United States banded together in a unique moment of unity following the September 11th terrorist attacks. The government was not responsible for this. The bad guys were. Together we would rebuild and attack. Then came Hurricane Katrina and we watched on international news as the storm's victims in New Orleans and the Gulf Coast waited on their rooftops for a government too disorganized and incompetent to save them. The war on terror was soon debunked as a war built on deception, and as terrorism intensified, we all wondered what the purpose was in all of this fighting. Then came the economic meltdown of 2008-09. While millions of Americans lost their homes and life savings, the biggest and most corrupt banks and businesses received billion-dollar rescue packages along with golden parachutes that allowed retiring CEOs to retreat in comfort and luxury. President Obama promised Americans a hope they could believe in, then further divided the country with programs and social engineering that held little prospect or positive impact for the average American. By 2016, America was not better off. It was simmering with anger and outrage from both sides of the political parties. The loss of trust has produced a perpetual state of anxiety and insecurity.

> *There is an evil I have seen under the sun, the sort of error that arises from a ruler: Fools are put in many high positions, while the rich occupy the low ones. I have seen slaves on horseback, while princes go on foot like slaves.*
> *Ecclesiastes 10:5-7*

Economic status is not an indicator of one's posture as a fool or a wise man. Today we see many fools in high positions. These are corrupt, usually well-off individuals who are in the role of decision makers and power brokers across the planet. Their decisions are often for sale. Their judgment is usually suspect. The promise of democracy once informed us that the most capable and deserving individuals would rise to the top of our societies and governments. These were the nobles who would rule and lead us through the dark times. If that was once true, it is no longer true today. Democracy has empowered the rise of fools to leadership positions. Sometimes this includes those most capable of orchestrating outrage and fear. At other times it includes those most capable of purchasing the will of the voters. The world is confronted by the reality that we no longer trust our leaders, but they are also the very leaders our society deserves. They reflect the will and heart of the people, dysfunctional and divided.

And in the face of the growing chaos, who is to say what is to come? It is one thing to manage the consistent flow from one bad news cycle to the next. As the population, food, and water crises intensify in their effects on terrorism, displaced people, coups, and civil wars, we can almost grow immune. The effects of consistent degeneration no longer shock us. But shocks will still come! The world is incredibly susceptible to disease and epidemic outbreaks today. What happens if an Ebola outbreak hits the east coast of the United States? What happens if a dirty bomb goes off in Tokyo? What happens if a high--profile assassination hits the next meeting of the G7? Does the world have the leadership infrastructure to confront such challenge?

No political answers or figureheads are coming to save us! As these type and level of events occur, it will not be a moment of recalibration and unity for the globe. With fools in high positions while princes go on foot, the world is not prepared for events that will serve as crisis multipliers.

1. Shah, Saeed. This article is more than 8 years old CIA organised fake vaccination drive to get Osama bin Laden's family DNA. *The Guardian.* [Online] July 11, 2011. [Cited: August 30, 2019.] https://www.theguardian.com/world/2011/jul/11/cia-fake-vaccinations-osama-bin-ladens-dna.
2. Katz, Jonathan M. New York Times. *U.N. Admits Role in Cholera Epidemic in Haiti.* [Online] August 17, 2016. [Cited: August 30, 2019.] https://www.nytimes.com/2016/08/18/world/americas/united-nations-haiti-cholera.html.

30

AS IT WAS IN THE DAYS OF NOAH

The world cannot endure another fifty years. The beginning of the end has already begun. My hope is that the pages of this book have demonstrated this reality to you, not as a doomsday prediction but a simple accumulation of facts. We are living in precarious times. Each day is filled with its own terrible stories of what is going on in the world -- wars and famine in one part of the world, mass shootings and rage in another part. This is what it looks like as the global system begins to collapse.

People will faint from terror, apprehensive of what is coming on the world.... Luke 21:26

It is not difficult to forecast what the coming months, years, and decades will hold. Resource wars will become more frequent. They will likely not be called that. In Syria, it was called a civil war; but in reality it was a war over a lack of resources and the unjust distribution that one class of power was seeking to implement at the disadvantage of others. The water crisis in the region occupied by the nuclear powers of Pakistan and India might fuel the next inflammation of resource scarcity so that it bursts out into full-fledged war.

Across the planet, wars and rumors of war will continue to increase, and the various geopolitical alliances will be pulled into the fights.

As the scarcity of resources intensifies and wars increase, so will their byproducts. Terrorism, displaced people, disease pandemics, coups, and failed states will continue to intrude into the normal day to day life of what it means to live at the end of the world. As the byproducts multiply, so will the countereffects. Domestic politics will become more fearful, more insecure, more capitalizing upon the insecurity of the people. Nationalists will grow more popular. Authoritarians will be given greater license. Yesterday's civil rights violations will be tomorrow's national security policies.

Social anxiety and unrest will continue to escalate. Our current levels of deaths of despair mentioned in an earlier chapter are only the beginning. Differing philosophies offered to explain the chaos and present solutions will proliferate, and opponents of those philosophies will be demonized and even criminalized. The social and cultural divisions and polarization we are seeing today are only the beginning. People will hold to their individual worldview as a matter of life or death and painfully oppose individuals and groups who disagree with them. This will not be an American phenomenon. It will be global: every tribe, tongue, and nation splintering in the divides of global fracture as the world comes undone.

> *Brother will betray brother to death, and a father his child. Children will rebel against their parents and have them put to death.* **Mark 13:12**

This is how the world ends. This is what is beginning and is coming. How then should we live in such a state of affairs? Should we be seeking out the solutions? Should we be seeking for governmental and global reform? Should we draw the world's attention to what is unfolding in hopes of extending the timeline of chaos?

Go Build an Ark

As Jesus looked to the end of time, he provided a hint of the model that those of us living at the end should follow.

> *As it was in the days of Noah, so it will be at the coming of the Son of Man. For in the days before the flood, people were eating and drinking, marrying and giving in marriage, up to the day Noah entered the ark; and they knew nothing about what would happen until the flood came and took them all away. That is how it will be at the coming of the Son of Man.*
> **Matthew 24:27-29**

Eschatology is the Biblical study of the end of the world. Differing schools of eschatological theories have used this passage of scripture to discern the timing of seasons and purposes of God, and in doing so missed the point. All scripture serves for us to learn more and be better equipped to live correctly in the midst of the circumstances God has placed us.

> *All Scripture is God-breathed and is useful for teaching, rebuking, correcting and training in righteousness,* **so that the servant of God may be thoroughly equipped for every good work.**
> **2 Timothy 3:16-17**

Jesus was letting us know how to respond to the chaos when living at the end of the world. There are plenty of other references by Jesus to what the end of time will look like so why talk about Noah here? It was not merely to describe what the end will look like but how the people of God should be postured when they arrive at the end of time.

> *Noah was a righteous man, blameless among the people of his time, and he walked faithfully with God. ¹⁰ Noah had three sons: Shem, Ham and Japheth.¹¹ Now the earth was corrupt in God's sight and was full of violence. ¹² God saw how corrupt the earth had become, for all the people*

on earth had corrupted their ways. ¹³ *So God said to Noah, "I am going to put an end to all people, for the earth is filled with violence because of them. I am surely going to destroy both them and the earth.*

Everything on earth will perish. ¹⁸ *But I will establish my covenant with you, and you will enter the ark—you and your sons and your wife and your sons' wives with you." Noah did everything just as God commanded him.*

Genesis 6:9-13, 17-18, 22

This passage from Genesis represents the times of Noah and how he responded in partnership with God to the end of the world.

- He lived righteously, distinct and unique from the corrupting generation he was born into.
- He recognized what was coming upon the earth and saw it as the inevitable will of God.
- His righteous stature gained him favor in the eyes of God, and God showed him the architecture of the ark (verses 14-16 describe the ark).
- The ark eventually preserved him and his home.
- That preservation was the foundation of a covenant with God (Genesis 9).

As we approach the end of the world, this is not the time for believers to be running to their caves and living as preppers. Noah lived correctly in the midst of his generation. His righteousness was in opposition to the prevailing trends of his age. He was a minority but he held to his belief in God's standard of truth, nonetheless. Today is not the time for the people of God to become fearful. It is a time where we must believe that we, like Noah, were born for this season.

Many argue that suggesting we are living at the end of the world today is a dangerous proposition. It gives cause for us to give up, to not look for solutions, to not be part of the answer to the world's problems all around us. That is not the case for Christian believers.

The end is to be an interruption of our daily life. Matthew 24 describes people working and going about their life as usual when they are suddenly interrupted. For believers going about our daily life means seeking to be the light of the world (Matthew 5:14). Where there is chaos, we should represent order. Where there is fear and anxiety, we should represent confidence and peace. We can do this in the midst of a collapsing order because our stability is drawn not from our environment but from the God we serve.

Most significantly, living at the end of the world is a time for the people of God, like Noah, to build an ark that will preserve their homes and their children and those whom they love. This is not a literal call to build a boat. It is a spiritual call to discern the architecture from God that will allow us to rise above the flows of chaos and crisis in this generation and stake our life upon that design. As the world trembles and shakes under the weight of one collapsing system after another, the people of God must live at a standard above it. While the earth filled with water, Noah and his house rode safely on the waves of the crisis. God does not hide these things, but He does require a pursuit of His will and preferences from His people. That is the manner by which He has always operated in order to draw us into partnership.

When the plagues were devasting Egypt in the book of Exodus the people of God looked to the designs and commands of God to learn how their families would be preserved. In the final plague, commemorated thereafter as Passover, the entire family and community of the Israelites were involved in the arrangement of the house, the order of the family, and the posture of every individual, obedient and ready to move at the impact of God. In Exodus 12 God outlines specific prescriptions for how each person among His people should carry themselves in the catastrophe that was about to befall the world they were living in. Consider what it was like to be a mother, a father, a son, a daughter in the presence of these commands. God was issuing the prescriptions for their preservation but also for their partnership with Him. When the end of the world arrives, God speaks and informs His people of His designs so they

can be both preserved and walk in closer alignment and partnership
to him.

What is the design of God for marriage? For raising and training
children? For doing business? For interacting with the world around
us? These are the elements of life which we must discern from scripture and a personal walk with God. These must be found within the
spiritual contexts of our churches. These Godly designs are the
instructions for the ark we must build to stay afloat in His purposes
while the rest of the earth is sinking in chaos.

The end of the world is coming. The end of the people of God is
not. Now is not the time to be hypnotized by the chaos into a state of
perpetual fear and anxiety.

> *But we do not belong to those who shrink back and are destroyed, but to
> those who have faith and are saved.* **Hebrews 10:39**

We were not called to fear or deception. We are called to take
hold of the purposes of God. We are called to know Him and His
ways. We are called to build His Kingdom -- first in our hearts, then in
our homes, then in the wider world around us!

> *The end of all things is near. Therefore, be alert and of sober mind so that
> you may pray. Above all, love each other deeply, because love covers over
> a multitude of sins. Offer hospitality to one another without grumbling.
> Each of you should use whatever gift you have received to serve others, as
> faithful stewards of God's grace in its various forms. If anyone speaks, they
> should do so as one who speaks the very words of God. If anyone serves,
> they should do so with the strength God provides, so that in all things God
> may be praised through Jesus Christ. To him be the glory and the power
> for ever and ever. Amen.* **1 Peter 4:7-11**

ABOUT THE AUTHOR

JB Shreve and his wife Casie live in northwest Arkansas with their three children Hudson, Elliott and Phoebe. They serve on the leadership team of The Community church. The Community is a part of Congress WBN's global network of churches.

Since 2012 JB Shreve has published more than 200 podcast episodes at www.theendofhistory.net. These podcasts are enjoyed by listeners around the world. They focus on world affairs and a biblical worldview - free of partisan political hype.

He also publishes an ongoing Intelligence Brief series which provide readers with concise and informed analysis of issues affecting the world. If you have enjoyed this book you might enjoy subscribing to JB's blog and also accessing his podcasts at Patreon.

Made in United States
North Haven, CT
13 May 2022

19158020R00126